Gossip

Filthy Rich

The Art of War

THE POWER PLAYS

George F. Walker

The Coach House Press   Toronto

Copyright © 1984, George F. Walker
Published with the assistance of the
Canada Council and the Ontario Arts Council.
These plays are fully protected by copyright.
All inquiries concerning performing rights,
professional or amateur, readings, or any other
use of this material should be directed to:
Great North Agency Limited
345 Adelaide Street West, Suite 500
Toronto, Ontario M5A 1V9

Cover photo: David Bolt as Tyrone M. Power in
Filthy Rich, Toronto Free Theatre, January 1979.

Photo credits:
Gossip. Robert C. Ragsdale, FRPS
Filthy Rich. Robert C. Ragsdale, FRPS
The Art of War. David Groskind, FRPS

Cover design: Gordon Robertson
Text design: Nelson Adams
Editor for the Press: Robert Wallace
The punctuation of these plays carefully adheres
to the author's instructions. The frequent omission of
question marks, for example, is deliberate.
Typeset in Zapf Book and printed in Canada
For a list of other books write for our
catalogue or call us at (416) 979-2217
The Coach House Press
401 (rear) Huron Street
Toronto, Canada M5S 2G5

Canadian Cataloguing in Publication
Walker, George F., 1947-
The power plays
Contents: Gossip – Filthy rich
– The art of war.
ISBN 0-88910-233-3
I. Title. II. Title: Gossip. III. Title: Filthy rich.
IV. Title: The art of war.
PS 8595.A 44 P 68 1984   C 812'.54   C 84-099522-9
PR 9199.3.W 34 P 68 1984

This book is dedicated to my wife, Susan Purdy

Contents

Introduction

1   This trilogy offers a very special kind of pleasure to the reader.

George F. Walker can cram a lot of extraordinary character and incident into a single play. So the sheer scope and range of three Walker plays, laid end to end, should be nothing less than breathtaking.

Sure enough, the Power Plays offer us an exhilarating parade of outrageous dramatic creations – from Brigot Nelson in *Gossip*, through Detective Stackhouse and Henry 'The Pig' Duvall in *Filthy Rich*, to Karla Mendez and General Hackman in *The Art of War*. And the action in each of these plays is full of wonderful surprises.

But the Power Plays also offer us the pleasures of familiarity and continuity. The unforgettable T.M. Power commands this trilogy. And by the end of *The Art of War*, Jamie McLean has become a good friend, too. We get to know these continuing characters much better than we could in a single play. And best of all, we get to watch them change and develop from one play to the next – as we watch the growth and development of Walker's work over the six-year period represented here.

Of course, the three plays are very different. But this trilogy has as much continuity as an honest biography – the kind that doesn't paper over the cracks between the passing years.

2   In *Gossip*, Power is a man with a job. He's an investigative journalist with a syndicated column. And the adventures of the play at first seem to be a vacation from his 'real' work. The structure of the play has a lot to do with the aesthetics of double-casting – an economic necessity in the kind of theatres that tend to premiere Walker's work – as the same few characters keep popping up in different

9

and exotic disguises. It's up to Power to penetrate those disguises and assess motives.

So, of the three plays, *Gossip*, is the most like a normal detective story. 'Who killed Bitch Nelson?' is the opening question. And the answer to that question is the parting shot. But unlike the normal detective, Power keeps so many of his ruminations and deductions to himself that we're invited to watch this menagerie of hypothetical villains bouncing off each other in the most hysterical and alarming ways.

At the centre of this ring of comic explosions, T.M. Power is like a reluctant stage manager with a deep dislike for the cast – setting demented traps for them, giving them unlikely scenes to play, and putting outrageous words into their mouths as he forces them to perform for an audience of their peers. Again unlike the normal detective, he seems motivated less by an heroic devotion to justice, than by a simple hatred of sham and flim-flam. To be perfectly frank, he's a bit of a misanthrope. And at the end of *Gossip*, we leave him drinking alone, having succeeded in putting away all the people he could reasonably regard as his friends.

3   At the start of *Filthy Rich*, we find Power once again drinking alone. Now, the hatred has been transmuted into self-hatred. And now, he's a man out of a job, dead drunk in a seedy tenement, trying to write a 'novel.' At the end of *Gossip*, Power's dog had died, and he's since replaced him with a less demanding, more melancholy pet – a bunch of fish living in an aquarium in the corner, where, on particularly bad days, Power goes to commune with nature.

Like Power's life, and like the fish, the plot of *Filthy Rich* is extremely slow-moving. Gone is the colourful out-of-fashion parade of *Gossip*. The whole first half of the play is devoted to Power's attempts to stay out of the detective story that threatens to involve him. When he does finally get involved, it's for two reasons – loyalty to an old friend, and the rude energy of Jamie McLean.

Jamie is the working-class hero of these plays. But

Walker's own working-class origins are too strong to let him get away with a cute stereotype. Jamie is usually very articulate, and always full of ambitious schemes. His young cynicism is both a perfect match and a perfect foil for Power's more well-aged bitterness. Best of all, their relationship is a continuing process of education for both of them, and they're both difficult students.

Power and Jamie have a few serious disagreements on the subject of money – which is, finally, the subject of the play. But in the end, the debate is overcome by an almost absurd kind of sadness, underscored by the nagging saxophonist outside Power's tenement window. And the closing scenes of the play are full of moments of something unspoken, sketching a set of unlikely bonds between Power and Stackhouse, between Jamie and Power, between Jamie and Susan, between Power and Anne.

In *Filthy Rich*, Power behaves even less like a normal detective than in *Gossip*. The plot is veiled in a melancholy haze. Several central characters never appear on stage, and one of them appears belatedly, in the form of a corpse. The business of detection is, as Power says, a simple 'process of elimination.' One of the Scott sisters is innocent, the other guilty. The plot see-saws gently between the two alternative hypotheses, as the Scott sisters perform their strange and mysterious double act.

4   At the end of *Filthy Rich*, Jamie tells Power, 'We need a bigger office.' At the time, he's pressing his luck. But in *The Art of War*, he gets his wish. Their 'office' is as big as all outdoors, as we meet them on the edge of a cliff somewhere in the wilderness of maritime Canada. A year and a half after *Filthy Rich*, Power is now a completely free agent, having abandonned even his troublesome 'novel.' He's nothing but a 'concerned citizen' now. And the play is not a detective story at all. We identify the villains in Scene 1, and learn what they're up to as soon as we get to know them. In fact, Walker calls the play an 'adventure.' And there is a hint of slightly superannuated Hardy Boys about this cliffside bivouac.

In *The Art of War*, Power finally gets to meet his true Moriarty – a nasty bit of business named Hackman. Like his antecedent in Sir Arthur Conan Doyle, Hackman needs Power's opposition almost as much as he needs to win. And at the end of the play, he looks forward to the pleasure of a return match, thus recognizing the epic stature of their relationship.

Thematically, *The Art of War* is the clearest of the Power Plays. Once again, Power's motivation is his loyalty to a fellow reporter. But here, his moral centre is articulated in a broader and more lucid fashion. He's somewhat ironically identified as a 'liberal.' And Hackman's chilling invocation of the 'vast darkness' of total war marks him as an emissary of neo-fascism. Their debate is the core of the play.

Power may be a 'liberal.' But Walker avoids the boring liberal view that 'art' and 'war' are opposites, the highest and lowest expressions of humanity. Instead, he shows how war goes hand in hand with a particular kind of art. Hackman represents them both, and with a vengeance.

The result is a kind of battle of styles. But Power's secret weapon is that he has no 'style' at all. In a social pinch, he can be relied on to 'drink the wine before the dinner,' to point the gun at the wrong angle, to think too long, or to say the first thing that pops into his head. Hackman, on the other hand, is all style, and very dangerous. The dynamics of this hilarious battle between art and artlessness take us to the heart of Walker's vision in this trilogy.

It's a vision in which true humanity is no match for inhumane craft. By the end of *The Art of War*, Power has achieved an important kind of self-awareness: 'Why can't we do anything properly?' he asks. And Jamie's need for a tragic ending is so strong, it actually blinds him to the reality of their final situation. It's a brilliant summation of the weakness of the 'liberal' point of view.

5 *The Art of War* was commissioned for a conference on the subject of 'Art and Reality.' And oddly enough, what it says on that subject provides an important insight into the

particular challenge of performing and directing these plays. The battle between the smooth art of Hackman and the bumpy reality of Power carries a clear implication that 'style' can be pernicious, even when it's most entertaining.

Power's life is not homogeneous. He's a creature of impulse and misdirection, candour and accidental emotion. As a result, the plays are not homogeneous. In a successful production of any of them, scenes of hysterical comedy are followed by scenes of strained seriousness. The only way to level out these plays, or to give them a conventional external shape, is to send them up.

But that would be to make them into Hackman's kind of theatre, rather than Power's – to make them into art for 'a discriminating society.' Hackman's favorite words are nouns like 'beauty' and 'style,' adjectives like 'tasteful' and 'arrogant.' These are not Power's kind of favourite words. And the 'art' they conjure up has no place in these plays. In performance, the Power Plays demand to be bumptious and fractious, calling up a whole range of reactions in no predictable order, rather than smooth and efficient, like Hackman's insidious 'art of war.' They are, after all, the Power plays. And like the man himself, their ability to surprise an audience into new recognitions about the world is their greatest strength.

6   Of course, it's also worth mentioning that the Power Plays are as funny as anything George F. Walker has ever written – and that's saying a lot. But on the whole, it's the kind of humour that comes from incongruity. And to really feel those moments of incongruity, you need to feel a healthy sense of reality about the characters, and their intentions, and the situations in which they find themselves.

Especially when you read these plays one after another, you can't help realizing that Walker is pretty particular about where those moments of incongruity have to occur. And that's what gives this trilogy its special coherence, through all its crazy diversity of plot and character.

It's a coherence that audiences should be able to enjoy

13

some day soon, when these three plays are finally together on the stage, performed in repertory as a genuine trilogy. In the meantime, this book brings them together in print, allowing the reader to experience them as the very substantial statement they are – a statement about life and art and many things in between. And that's a special kind of pleasure indeed.

William Lane.
Toronto, October 1983.

Gossip

Gossip was first produced at Toronto Free Theatre, Toronto, in May 1977, with the following cast:

T.M. POWER. David Bolt
BAXTER. Jim Henshaw
PETER BELLUM. Stephen Markle
ANNA. Ilana Frank
ALLAN. Geofferey Bowes
BRIGOT NELSON. Meg Hogarth
MARGARET. Wendy Thatcher
NORMAN LEWIS. Ian Beckthorpe
SAM LEWIS. Maury Chaykin

Directed by John Palmer
Sets and Costumes by Martin Johnson
Music composed and played
by Phillip Schreibman.

Persons in the Play
T.M. POWER
BAXTER
PETER BELLUM
ANNA
ALLAN
BRIGOT NELSON
MARGARET
NORMAN LEWIS
SAM LEWIS
SUSAN LONG
PEDRO PUCHINSKY

*Intermission should come between
Scenes Eight and Nine.*

Scene One

A small crowd of elegantly dressed people. Gathered around a rubber tire which is suspended from the ceiling by an old rope. The people are staring at the tire. Looking appreciative. Smiling stupidly. They are all holding champagne glasses. A dull roar of small talk. We hear the odd 'significant' word. Finally a lady raises her glass. Silence.

LADY A toast. [*They all raise their glasses.*] To minimal art!

ALL Oh!! [*They drink. They look at the tire again. The lady who proposed the toast falls through the tire. Dead.*]
BLACKOUT

Scene Two

T.M. POWER in a spotlight. The man is middle-aged and balding. He wears glasses, an old poorly-fitted suit and a bow tie. He is staring into space. Eventually, he squints his eyes, as is his custom when something is bothering him.

POWER Who killed Bitch Nelson? [*A long pause. He squints his eyes again.*] And who the hell cares? [*Lights up on the rest of the stage. A desk, a couple of chairs. Enough to suggest an office in a newspaper building.* BAXTER *the editor is leaning over the desk looking at* POWER's *back. He holds a submarine sandwich in one hand, a pint of milk in the other.*]

BAXTER Lots of people care, Power. Our readers care. And when they care, I care.

POWER [*pounds his knuckles into his chest*]. I'm a political journalist. I write about politics. I do not investigate the

17

murders of celebrities. For that you need a police reporter
or a gossip columnist. I am neither. I am a political
journalist!

BAXTER Stop shouting at me. I'm your boss. Try to show at least a
token amount of respect.

POWER Then stop bothering me with this crap! I'm on the verge of
cracking open the biggest political scandal this country
has ever seen. I've got three separate cases of kickbacks to
look into, a federal budget which doesn't make any sense
at all and a cabinet minister who can barely spell his own
name making policy statements about foreign affairs.

BAXTER Bad news. That's all we ever get from you. I think you've
become a nihilist.

POWER Listen, you goddamn moron, all I'm doing is giving the
facts.

BAXTER Don't call me a goddamn moron, Power. I'm your
goddamn boss.

POWER You're my goddamn boss because your old man bought
this newspaper on a whim. A whim. He could have just as
easily bought a hockey team and made you a puck. May he
rot in eternal hell.

BAXTER Only one kind of person could talk like that about a dead
man who gave him his first and only job. A nihilist.

POWER Jesus Christ. All right. I'm a nihilist. So what?

BAXTER People are bored with bad news. They don't want to read
that the world is falling apart every day. They want to read
about other things.

POWER Like what?

BAXTER Personalities. Celebrities. Who poisoned one of the
biggest celebrities of all. Which one of those personalities at the minimal art gallery did it. Who killed Bitch
Nelson.

POWER I don't care.

BAXTER Exactly. You have the best possible attitude for
investigative reporting. Indifference. Besides, I want to
give those poor suckers who read your little doom report
a bit of a break. I mean what exactly is it that you think you
write about?

POWER What's that supposed to mean?

BAXTER In the last two weeks you've used the word cataclysm
eighteen times, anathema eleven times and, get this,

Armageddon twenty-six times. In short you are writing about the end of the world.

POWER So what?

BAXTER Well it's depressing.

POWER What exactly would you run in place of my column?

BAXTER Gossip.

POWER You mean stuff like 'What TV producer takes his script girl to Hawaii between takes?'

BAXTER Or what cabinet minister's sister has rejected a well-known political journalist in favour of the cabinet minister himself?

POWER That's below the belt.

BAXTER It sells newspapers. It pays your salary.

POWER You're sick, Baxter. You're star struck. I've seen the kind of magazines you read. *People, Celebrity, Motion Picture Mirror.*

BAXTER I like stories about famous people.

POWER You like mindless prattle about people with expensive hair cuts.

BAXTER I don't want to hear any more of your dirty nihilistic double-talk. I just want you to find the murderer.

POWER All right. I'll try reason with you. You've heard of reason, eh? That's what you use when you *think.* You've heard of thinking, eh?!

BAXTER Don't patronize me, Power. It's bad for our relationship.

POWER The police haven't been able to find the murderer. It's been six months. No arrests. Not even any suspects. What makes you think I can do better?

BAXTER You're smarter than they are.

POWER Right. I quit.

BAXTER You can't quit. You signed a lifetime contract with this paper.

POWER I was drunk when I signed it. Your father got me drunk. The immoral son of a bitch. I'll get out of it.

BAXTER You've tried three times to get out of it. Give up, Power. The contract's air-tight. You work for me or you don't work for anybody.

POWER Fine. I'll write my novel.

BAXTER Your novel is the joke of the whole newspaper.

POWER No, it's only the joke of the fifteenth floor. You're the joke of the whole newspaper. [*Pause.*] Listen, Baxter, this isn't like you. You're behaving almost evangelically about this Bitch Nelson thing. Do you have some sort of personal stake in it?

BAXTER   Look, Bitch Nelson was news. More than a politician. More than a scientist. She was a rich celebrity. An eccentric. And in her own way, a star. The people care about stars, Power. Think of it this way. I'm asking you to do this for the people.

POWER   Tell the people I quit.

BAXTER   No you don't.

POWER   Yes I do.

BAXTER   No. You take six weeks. You find out who poisoned the Bitch. And then you get your column back. [POWER *has turned away.*] Well?

POWER   Get out of my office. This is my office.

BAXTER   Here's a list of people who were at the gallery the night she was murdered. [*Puts it on the desk.*] Remember. Six weeks. [BAXTER *leaves.* POWER *watches him go. Then goes to his chair behind the desk. Sits. Puts his feet on the desk.*]

POWER   Six weeks. [*Pause.*] I'll do it in one. [*He reaches for the telephone.*]

BLACKOUT

Scene Three

Rehearsal hall. Two young actors, one female, one male, are moving around. Mumbling things. PETER BELLUM, *a British stage director in his mid-thirties, is watching them. Moving around on the periphery of their activity.* POWER *is sitting on a chair. Head in his palm. More or less watching* BELLUM *watch the actors.*

BELLUM   Keep moving. Claim your space. Define it. [*Actors are moving around eyeing each other with hostility.*] Don't stop. Keep moving. Look for your space. Create activity. [ANNA *pushes the male actor.*] Good. Very good, indeed. Now verbalize your imperative. So that Allan must respond.

ANNA [*pushes the actor again*]. You cause me pain. You live in slime. I'm gonna castrate you. Then I'm gonna get a divorce.

BELLUM Good. The aesthetic is domestic violence. Create an activity. [ANNA *grabs the actor by the crotch. Male actor screams. Grabs his crotch.*]

ALLAN God, Peter. She hurt me.

BELLUM Her imperative. You should have kept it going.

ALLAN I'm in pain.

BELLUM Oh stop it, Allan. I am not interested in your pain unless you define it in the context. Break! [*The actors wander off. BELLUM sits down beside* POWER.]

BELLUM One of the hazards of using non-Equity actors. Not much technique.

POWER There's a technique for having your crotch grabbed?

BELLUM [*Picks up a thermos. Pours some tea into a cup.*] Certainly. Brando wouldn't have flinched. He would have just internalized the whole thing and turned it into one of those magic moments in theatre. Tea?

POWER No thanks. I want to talk about that night at the art gallery.

BELLUM Very well. But I'd rather discuss aesthetics.

POWER Some other time, maybe.

BELLUM Whenever. I'm usually here.

POWER Well, Mr. Bellum, I know –

BELLUM Call me Peter.

POWER I know the police have probably asked you this, but did you see anything?

BELLUM Oh plenty. They're a very strange crowd you know.

POWER Specifically. Did you see anything which might pertain to Miss Nelson's death?

BELLUM Well, how is one to know what pertains and what doesn't. I saw a certain amount of activity. Normal personal expression. Some deviation from normal personal expression. Et cetera.

POWER Et cetera?

BELLUM Mostly sexual. They're a very active crowd that way.

POWER They?

BELLUM I'm not really one of them. I received an invitation. I went. Mostly because I admire the artist who was being exhibited. Pedro Whatshisname.

POWER Pedro Puchinsky.

21

BELLUM Yes. Very whimsical. Rubber tires indeed. Great stuff. Anyway, I'm not a regular in that crowd.

POWER And your relationship with Miss Nelson.

BELLUM She admired my work from afar. Eventually she got closer. When she was close enough I put the bite on her bank book. She had a considerable bank book.

POWER Sex?

BELLUM Yes, I suppose she had one of those as well. Take your own guess as to which though. Oh smile now. You can't be all that serious about it.

POWER Was your relationship with her ever sexual?

BELLUM I'm a faggot.

POWER Oh.

BELLUM Oh, he says. I hope this isn't going to change your attitude towards me. I was hoping we'd get the chance to talk sometime. I have read your column for quite a while and I'm fascinated by your lack of irony.

POWER Oh.

BELLUM Oh, he says again.... Probably thinking what does he know. Stupid queer.

POWER No. I was thinking about my fascinating lack of irony. I don't usually spend much time thinking about stupid queers.

BELLUM Quite right too. But I'm a British faggot. There's quite a difference between a British faggot and a North American faggot.

POWER What is it?

BELLUM Upbringing.

POWER Of course.

BELLUM A more dignified approach is what I'm talking about. Less direct abuse. More innuendo. When you look at a North American faggot you're looking at someone who has probably been referred to at least once in his life as a 'homo'. Disgusting sound to that word isn't there? Homo. Always brings the same picture to mind. A drooling hunchback in a boy's gymnasium. I much prefer 'queer'. But then I'm a classicist. Did you know that William Blake was a homosexual?

POWER [*groans*]. He was not.

BELLUM Oh, stop it. Of course he was. *Songs of Innocence* indeed!

Then of course there was Augustus John. Surrounded by all those women all the time. They were gypsies of course, but even so. So many women. Too many if you think about it.

POWER Are you thinking about it now?

BELLUM No. I was thinking about Elvis Presley.

POWER Can we talk about something else.

BELLUM Certainly. What?

POWER Any thoughts you might have on who could have killed Miss Nelson.

BELLUM I know nothing. I could speculate if I had to. As to motive. Opportunity. The usual.

POWER Go ahead.

BELLUM Speculation is a dangerous business. Especially when it involves such very influential people. I didn't do it for the police and although I'm trying awfully hard I can't think of a reason to do it for you.

POWER My paper is about to appoint a new drama critic, a friend of mine who owes me a favour. Some speculation from you, a good review from my friend.

BELLUM The implication being that I need outside assistance in order to achieve good reviews. What an incredibly obscene and yet somehow deeply typical and fundamentally grotesque North American heterosexual insult.

POWER I withdraw the offer.

BELLUM Don't be rash. I've been insulted before. Let me think about it. And if I agree I'll write it all down and send it along anonymously. Fair?

POWER Sure.

BELLUM [*Starts off. Stops.*] However here's a little something to keep you busy in the meantime. Her sister, Brigot Nelson the poetess. Go see her. And if you get the chance mention Argentina of all places and see if that gets a rise. [POWER *nods casually.* BELLUM *leaves.* POWER *leans back in his chair, hands on his head. After a moment* ANNA *comes in. Sipping coffee from a plastic cup.*]

ANNA Well, did you like what we were doing?

POWER Not much. What's it called anyway?

ANNA Garbage. Everything I do is called garbage. Eventually I'll

have to take my sweater off. Then it will be called garbage
with tits. Give me your card.

POWER What do you mean?

ANNA All detectives have a card.

POWER I'm not a detective. [*Reaches into his pocket.*] How about if
I just write my number down on this Kleenex. [*He does.
Gives it to her.*]

ANNA Can you pay for information?

POWER I guess so.

ANNA I'll tell you the truth, mister. I need money pretty bad. This
is a big city and I'm just a little girl trying to hold my own.

POWER Try to be more specific.

ANNA Well, I overheard you talking to Peter. I was at the art
gallery that night too.

POWER I'm listening.

ANNA I'll be in touch with you soon. It's a long story. I need more
time to tell it. [*She leaves.* BELLUM *comes back on. Peeling
an orange.*]

BELLUM Still here?

POWER No. [*Stands. Leaves.* BELLUM *picks up a telephone. Dials.*]

BELLUM It's me. The rumours were true. He's on the case. You're
going to kill him. When? At your leisure. Oh. Why should I
be nervous? You're the one who should be nervous. Oh
yes, I forgot. I guess I should be nervous too. All right, what
should I do? I don't want to do that. It's dangerous. No, I
don't want to do that either. That's more dangerous. What
do you mean it's all relative. Relative to what? No, I've
never had that experience. No, I don't particularly wish to.
Yes, you've made your point. [*Hangs up.*] Oh dear [*Eats a
piece of orange.*]

BLACKOUT

Scene Four

Begins in darkness. POWER *is moving cautiously about. We
hear a rhythmic creaking sound.*

POWER Hello? Is anyone here? [*Lights a match. Keeps moving.*

Suddenly trips over something. Falls. Match goes out. Darkness.] Ah, for Christ's sake.

BRIGOT What do you want?

POWER Can we have some light?

BRIGOT No. What do you want?

POWER I want some light.

BRIGOT Light. Okay. Here it is. [*A small lamp is turned on.*] Light. Big deal. [BRIGOT NELSON *is sitting in a rocking chair next to a small table where the lamp sits. Rocking slowly back and forth. She is a striking angular woman. Wearing sunglasses, wrapped in a shawl. Her hands firmly grasp the arms of the rocker. Fingers outstretched.* POWER *is sitting on the floor looking at her very closely.*]

BRIGOT You're staring. [*Reaches over and turns off the lamp. Darkness.*]

POWER [*groans*]. Oh, for Christ's sake. I don't need this. I can sell the car. Go away. Write my book.

BRIGOT Shut up.

POWER What was that?

BRIGOT I'm not interested in listening to your interior monologues. If you have something important to say, say it. Then get out.

POWER I want to talk about your sister's death.

BRIGOT That's not important. Goodbye [*pause*].

POWER Okay. Then let's talk about Argentina. [*Lamp is turned on.* BRIGOT *is staring at* POWER *now.*]

BRIGOT How did you get in here?

POWER Your houseboy let me in. [BRIGOT *rings a little bell.* ALLAN *enters wearing a houseboy's jacket.*]

ALLAN Yes, Miss Nelson.

BRIGOT Did you let this man in?

ALLAN Yes, Miss Nelson.

BRIGOT And why did you do that?

ALLAN He bribed me.

BRIGOT With how much?

ALLAN Twelve dollars.

BRIGOT Loyalty is cheap, isn't it? Why didn't you ask for more?

ALLAN Twelve dollars was all I needed. That's how much tonight's acting class costs.

BRIGOT I had a vision last night, Allan. A new world was upon us.

The enslaved were free, the corrupt were purged, the
lethargic were inspired and the actors were gone. What
do you think of that?

ALLAN   I think that's sad. Acting is all I want to do, Miss Nelson.

BRIGOT   In the new world there won't be any acting. Just reality.
You are dismissed.

ALLAN   Does that mean I'm fired? [BRIGOT *goes over. Puts her arms
around him affectionately.*]

BRIGOT   No, you sadly deficient little man, it only means that you
are to leave the room for a while or I might not be able to
control myself. I might reach over and pull your face off.
[ALLAN *nods. Leaves.*]

POWER   That reminds me. I forgot to feed my dog.

BRIGOT   Who are you?

POWER   Name is Power.

BRIGOT   Question was not What is your name. Question was, Who
are you. Now answer it!

POWER   Press.

BRIGOT   I don't talk to the press. They distort my words. Stress the
negative. I despise the press.

POWER   I don't really care.

BRIGOT   You should [*Slaps him.*]

POWER   Why did you do that?

BRIGOT   Impulse. I sometimes lose control. I apologize. do you
accept? That was a question. Answer it. [*She swings. He
catches her arm. Holds it.*]

POWER   Listen. Can we cut the shit?

BRIGOT   Who told you about Argentina?

POWER   Me first! [*They stare at each other.*]

BRIGOT   Go ahead. But be careful. [*He lets her go. Pause.*]

POWER   According to the police reports you refused to answer any
questions concerning your sister's death. Why is that?

BRIGOT   Wasn't interested.

POWER   I find that difficult to believe.

BRIGOT   Are you familiar with my work?

POWER   You're a poet.

BRIGOT   Close. I'm a prophet. Never mind that though. If you'd
read my work and if you had any kind of sensibility you'd
understand why I'm not interested in my sister, her death

or any of her 'friends'. My work is pragmatic. Concerned.
My sister and her crowd were superficial.

POWER Nevertheless.

BRIGOT Nevertheless nothing. In order to create an artist closes off
what is of no consequence. Milk deliveries. Heavy
snowfalls. Sisters. Jane and I never had much in common.
She was a little rich girl who married little rich boys. She
never had a purpose. Never had a vocation. One day she'd
be trying painting, the next, interior decorating. Acting in
plays. Producing plays. Giving money to all sorts of
insignificant people to do insignificant things. I suppose
she thought she was making friends. The wrong kind,
obviously.

POWER One of her friends killed her?

BRIGOT Of course.

POWER Any ideas who it might be?

BRIGOT None that I wish to share with you.

POWER Look, there's a killer still running around out there, lady.

BRIGOT Not likely to kill again. Probably a crime of passion. She
had dozens of affairs.

POWER It was probably a man then.

BRIGOT Not necessarily.

POWER Are you saying she was bisexual?

BRIGOT That was vicious gossip.

POWER But you said –

BRIGOT Oh, why dwell on little things. Use your position to look
ahead for those who can't. Change. Improve. Build new
structures.

POWER I'm more interested in digging up termites in the old
structures. Why are you looking at me like that?

BRIGOT Yes. You were in one of my visions. I just remembered. The
new world was upon us. Everyone was busy contributing
to the common blissful goal. Everyone except you. You
were on the outside nagging and complaining. Eventually
you turned to dust.

POWER Yeah. That makes sense. So you have visions.

BRIGOT Yes.

POWER That's quite unusual.

BRIGOT Well, of course it's unusual, you fool.

POWER	No need to be insulting.
BRIGOT	I'll be the judge of that.
POWER	I'll make a deal. You tell me who you think killed your sister and I won't tell your public that you're a cranky old broad who thinks she has visions.
BRIGOT	I don't have a public. I have a cult. Now who told you about Argentina?
POWER	Peter Bellum.
BRIGOT	[*chuckles*]. That silly little theatre director with the store-bought Oxford accent. Then it's nothing. Just gossip. How embarrassing to be conned by the likes of you. Get out of here before I catch my second wind.
POWER	Just one more question. How do you reconcile your 'concern' and your visions of a 'better world' with your use of violence and your miserable personality?
BRIGOT	Like this. [*She reaches over. Turns off the lamp. Darkness.*]

Scene Five

POWER's *office.* BAXTER *is sitting on the edge of the desk. Eating a submarine sandwich. Reading* People *magazine.* POWER *comes in. Taking off his jacket. Loosening his tie.*

POWER	What are you doing in my office?
BAXTER	Waiting for you.
POWER	Stay out of my office. There's always a bad feeling in the air when you leave. It takes me hours to overcome it.
BAXTER	What's Brigot Nelson like?
POWER	Later, Baxter.
BAXTER	Is it true that she's a cross between Gertrude Stein and Jane Fonda?
POWER	[*throws him a dirty look*]. She has visions about a new world. She has a houseboy who takes acting lessons with Peter Bellum. She didn't like her sister. She didn't like her sister's friends. She spends her time in dark rooms and she's a violent schizophrenic. Amazing, eh.
BAXTER	But what's it all mean?

28

POWER I haven't got the slightest idea.

BAXTER Well, do you think it's important?

POWER I sincerely hope not, Baxter.

BAXTER Do you think it's going to help you find the murderer?

POWER No. But it's made me curious. She was really shaken when I mentioned Argentina. I might as well find out why. [POWER *is casually reading his mail.*]

BAXTER I think Argentina is a red herring. You should interrogate the houseboy.

POWER Are you telling me how to conduct my investigation?

BAXTER No. I'm giving you my advice.

POWER Your advice is absolutely last on my list of immediate needs.

BAXTER You like me a lot, don't you? I mean you only talk to me with such contempt because it's part of your persona. Right?

POWER Yeah. When I go home at night and drop my persona I always think of you in a different way.

BAXTER I thought so.

POWER Ah, leave me alone. Civilization is sinking into the slime and I'm running around interviewing the fringe element.

BAXTER Admit it, Power. You're having a wonderful time.

POWER You think so, eh. Take a look at this. [*Hands him one of the pieces of correspondence he has gone through.* BAXTER *reads it. Looks up slowly.*]

BAXTER Now who would be threatening your life? [POWER *shrugs.*] Should we call the police?

POWER What are they going to do? Trace the crayon?

BAXTER They could give you protection.

POWER In my whole life I've only wanted protection from two people. You and your late father.

BAXTER Leave my father out of this.

BOTH He was a great man!

POWER What is this unhealthy obsession you have with your father's reputation? Why don't you ever talk about your mother?

BAXTER I loved my mother. She was an amazing lady. She helped build the art gallery.

POWER [*smiles*]. She was a construction worker?

BAXTER No. She was a fund-raiser.

POWER	I knew one of those once. Spent all day on the phone being charming to total strangers. Then went home and beat up her children.
BAXTER	I was wrong about you, Power. You're not a nihilist. You just don't like people. I'm going home.
POWER	Here are the keys to my apartment. Will you stop off and feed my dog?
BAXTER	Does he bite?
POWER	The poor bastard is fourteen years old. He can hardly walk.
BAXTER	[*Starts off. Turns back.*] Oh, I forgot. You've got a visitor. Margaret.
POWER	Where is she?
BAXTER	Washroom. I thought it was over between you two.
POWER	'It?' What's an 'it', Baxter? Margaret and I were friends. We used to talk a lot.
BAXTER	About what?
POWER	Her brother, mostly.
BAXTER	Sure. You get personal info on one of the country's most important politicians and you never use it?
POWER	[*throws him a look*]. Confidential, Baxter.
BAXTER	Talk. [*Laughs.*] Sure. [*Leaves.*]
POWER	Feed my dog! [*He picks up the threat letter which* BAXTER *has left on the desk. Reads it.* MARGARET *comes in. A beautiful lady. Mid-twenties. Trenchcoat. Tinted glasses. Kerchief. She has brought him a rose. She puts it in his typewriter. He looks at her. The rose. Turns away. She goes to him. Begins to gently massage his temples. A moment's silence.*]
MARGARET	You don't seem very excited about seeing me.
POWER	I thought you were never coming back.
MARGARET	All the more reason for you to be thrilled that I'm here. [*No response.*] Well, at least tell me how I look. Do I look good?
POWER	You always look good. Maybe if you'd show up sometime looking just a bit mediocre.
MARGARET	Come on, smile, Tyrone.
POWER	Please. Don't call me that.
MARGARET	Sorry. Forgot.
POWER	How is your brother these days? Consummated any childhood dreams lately?

Scene Five

MARGARET Paul was in South America last month.

POWER That man will go anywhere to have his picture taken. Must have been hard for you to get sleep with him gone. [*She starts off.*] Keep going, Margaret. Don't stop. [*She stops.*]

MARGARET I didn't come here to talk about my relationship with Paul.

POWER In the three years I've known you you've never talked about anything else.

MARGARET You talk about him as much as I do.

POWER But for different reasons. Everything he does is so meaningless. So much money. So much power. And nothing but gestures. It's like performing Shakespeare in a desert. Shakespeare. What the hell am I talking about Shakespeare for? My mind is rotting away.

MARGARET I'm here on a shopping trip. I plan to get my hair done. Visit the museum. See a few plays. Go dancing. Have a really wonderful time then check myself into the psychiatric hospital. [*Smiles.*] I think maybe I can avoid that last activity if you'll let me stay with you while I'm here. [POWER *mumbles something.*] Good. [*Takes off her coat. Sits behind the desk.*] Let me know when you're ready to go. [POWER *mumbles something twice.*] Baxter tells me you're investigating the Jane Nelson murder.

POWER More or less.

MARGARET A strange lady.

POWER You knew her?

MARGARET Met her at a party once, at the Danish embassy. An odd evening. All these healthy-looking Scandinavians walking around looking so chipper then disappearing into the bathroom to slit their wrists. Why do you suppose they have such a high suicide rate?

POWER They're very courageous people. Jane Nelson?

MARGARET She worked on my brother's last campaign. It was such a difficult campaign, Tyrone. So many pressures. I just don't think I can go through any –

POWER Later. What do you mean she worked on his campaign. What did she do?

MARGARET She gave him money.

POWER How much?

MARGARET I don't know. What's it matter?

David Bolt (T.M. POWER) and Wendy Thatcher (MARGARET).

POWER There are limits on personal campaign contributions.

MARGARET Come off it, Tyrone. No one takes that seriously.

POWER How much?

MARGARET I don't know! Stop trying to get at Paul. I think you only do it because you can't stand the fact that he's got everything you haven't. Popularity. Purpose. Respect.

POWER You! [*They turn away from each other.*] Never mind. I'll find out myself.

MARGARET I'm sorry I said that. You do have virtues of your own. They're just a bit vague, that's all. How will you find out?

POWER Her lawyers. I have to talk to them anyway.

MARGARET The Lewis brothers?

POWER You know them too?

MARGARET Only by reputation.

POWER Which is?

MARGARET Brutal. Devious. A bit kinky. I wouldn't go there unprepared.

POWER I wasn't intending to. I have some friends out doing some research on them for me right now.

MARGARET Have you found out anything yet?

POWER No.

MARGARET Well it was just a simple murder. Probably a crime of passion.

POWER What makes you say that?

MARGARET That's what they're saying in the capital.

POWER What else are they saying in the capital?

MARGARET Just that you are all washed up as a columnist.

POWER Really? Is that right? Is that so? Goddamn rumour mongers. Insidious leeches. Good. That's just what I needed to hear. [*Hurriedly puts on his shoes. Grabs his coat.*]

MARGARET Aren't you interested in hearing what I need?

POWER I used to be.

MARGARET I need someone to talk to. Someone to hear all about the tension in my life. Such an incredible amount of tension. Paul is always away. Magazines have stopped buying my poetry. Gossip columnists are always making snide remarks about the fact that I'm inherently useless. I just don't know what I have to do to prove –

POWER Later. Please. Later. [*He starts off.*]

MARGARET	Where are you going?
POWER	I've got a murder to solve.
MARGARET	[*stands*]. I don't want to be alone.
POWER	Then go out and buy yourself a friend. [POWER *leaves.* MARGARET *starts after him.*]
	BLACKOUT

Scene Six

NORMAN *and* SAM LEWIS. *Brothers. Middle-aged. Sitting up in bed. Sitting between them with the covers up to her chin is* ANNA, *the young actress.* POWER *is standing about ten feet from the bed. Expressionless. Holding a pile of papers.*

POWER	The door was open.
NORMAN	The door is always open.
POWER	You said, come in.
SAM	We always say, come in.
ANNA	And someone always does. [*Waves.*] Hi, Power. [POWER *waves.*] Well I guess I'll get changed. [*She gets out of bed. She is wearing a vinyl body stocking. Very shiny. As she is passing* POWER *she notices his curious look.*] It's a job. [POWER *nods.* ANNA *leaves. Pause.* SAM *and* NORMAN *point to a chair near the bed.*]
BOTH	Sit down. [POWER *goes to the chair. Smiles a little. Sits.*]
NORMAN	Cigarette?
POWER	No thanks.
NORMAN	I meant, have you got a cigarette?
POWER	Oh. Sure. [POWER *takes out a pack of cigarettes. Offers it to* NORMAN. NORMAN *takes a cigarette.*]
NORMAN	What about my brother? [POWER *nods. Offers* SAM *the pack.* SAM *takes a cigarette.* POWER *sits.*] Light? [POWER *sighs. Takes out a lighter. Stands. Lights their cigarettes.*]
POWER	Anything else?
NORMAN	Sit down. [POWER *sits. They are staring at him.* POWER *doesn't appear to have a thought in his head. He is smiling almost stupidly. A long, almost peaceful silence. Finally,*

SAM, *reaching over* NORMAN, *extends his hand to* POWER.]

SAM My name is Sam Lewis.

POWER [*Shakes* SAM's *hand.*] Hello.

SAM My brother, Norman Lewis. [NORMAN *and* POWER *shake.* POWER *sits back. Another long silence.* SAM *and* NORMAN *look at each other. They look at* POWER.]

BOTH What's your name?

POWER Excuse me for a minute, will you? [*He stands. Leaves.* SAM *and* NORMAN *look at each other. Lights out in that area. Lights up on another area adjacent.* POWER *is pacing back and forth.* MARGARET *is watching him.*] Do you still carry that flask of scotch?

MARGARET I don't know what you mean.

POWER Please. Not now, Margaret. I need a drink.

MARGARET [*reaching into her purse*]. I only use it for times of great stress. The last time I used it was in Japan when the diplomatic corps wouldn't let me give my poems to the emperor. I was so hurt. So tense.

POWER Later, Margaret. [*Takes the flask. Drinks.*] Those guys in there run one of the biggest law firms in the country. And they're very weird, Margaret. They share a bed with a teenage girl in a vinyl body stocking and they sometimes talk in unison.

MARGARET My psychiatrist would say perversion is passé as a serious emotional problem.

POWER I was paralyzed.

MARGARET My psychiatrist would say you were responding to your own dubious sexuality.

POWER There's nothing dubious about my sexuality, Margaret. I just don't have a sexuality. You took it away from me on your last visit.

MARGARET How can we be friends when you have an attitude like that?

POWER Look, all I'm saying is that since you rejected me sexually, I've had certain problems with my confidence in that area. And naturally I blame you.

MARGARET You used to be such a good listener.

POWER Jesus Christ!

MARGARET Why are you shouting?

POWER You're driving me crazy.

MARGARET   Let's talk about it.

POWER   We'll talk about it later. I mean you'll talk. I'll listen. Right now I have to deal with the Lewis Brothers. They're supposed to be protecting Jane Nelson's interests. My sources tell me half of her estate is missing.

MARGARET   Are you saying they killed her?

POWER   My sources also tell me Norman Lewis once disappeared for about a month. And where did he turn up? Argentina of all places.

MARGARET   So what?

POWER   Argentina. What is all this Argentina stuff?

MARGARET   You're supposed to be solving a murder.

POWER   But there's no reason I can't enjoy myself by getting those bastards and maybe some of their big-shot friends while I'm at it.

MARGARET   You're a sadist.

POWER   What?

MARGARET   People in high places sometimes have to do things that aren't exactly legal. You don't have to persecute them for it.

POWER   You've been living in the capital too long, Margaret.

MARGARET   I know. [*She grabs him.*] Help me!

POWER   Listen. Did your brother ever work with Norman and Sam?

MARGARET   Stop trying to implicate Paul in everything. You're just going to make yourself look stupid.

POWER   Poor old Paul.

MARGARET   It's not Paul I'm worrying about. It's you.

POWER   Oh please, Margaret. You can't say things like that to me when I'm conscious. I hear them.

MARGARET   Okay. But unless you want to fall on your face, stick to the murder. Ask them about Pedro Puchinsky. He's the prime suspect. He was having an affair with Jane Nelson. She dumped him.

POWER   How do you know that?

MARGARET   Common knowledge.

POWER   Really. I must be reading the wrong magazines.

MARGARET   Just find out about Pedro. Trust me.

POWER   I'll think about it. [*Hands her the flask.*] Here's your friend. [*Turns around.*] May I come in?

Scene Six

NORMAN Yes. [*Lights out on this area as* POWER *takes a step forward. Lights up on the area where* SAM *and* NORMAN *are. They are both dressed in very distinguished dark suits.* SAM *is sitting very formally in the chair.* NORMAN *is standing to one side. His arms behind his back.* POWER *is entering.*]

NORMAN Yes. Please do come in. Take a chair. Samuel. [SAM *rises. Gestures toward the chair.* POWER *inches his way there slowly. Eyeing them both.*]

NORMAN Now, who are you and what exactly is your business here?

POWER My name is Power. I'm with the press.

NORMAN Power. The columnist?

POWER Yes.

NORMAN Identification. [POWER *produces a card.*] Samuel. [SAM *retrieves the card.*]

SAM Appears to be legitimate.

NORMAN Well what is it then, Mr. Power. It's late. We don't usually do business in our home.

ANNA [*Comes walking through briskly, doing up her coat. Takes some money from* SAM's *outstretched hand without breaking her stride.*] Goodnight. [*to* POWER] There's more there than you'll first suppose. I'll call you. [*She leaves.*]

POWER Jane Nelson's estate.

SAM What about it?

POWER Half of it is missing. [SAM *looks at* NORMAN. NORMAN *avoids his look.*]

NORMAN Nonsense.

POWER I have the proof right here.

NORMAN [*pointing*]. Samuel. [SAM *goes over. Looks over* POWER's *shoulder.* POWER *flips a few sheets for him.*]

SAM Yes. Our letterhead. Photocopies of Miss Nelson's files.

NORMAN Where did you get those?

POWER I've been in my business a long time. I have sources. Friends.

NORMAN Criminals.

SAM Thieves.

POWER Let's just call them back alley artists. That way you'll appreciate them more. You're both art patrons.

NORMAN We could have you arrested.

POWER [*holds up the papers*]. I could put you out of business. [*Pause.*]

SAM The man is a swine, Norman. He is obviously capable of some very low-brow behaviour.

POWER I don't have any class at all.

NORMAN To be sure. But do you know who you're dealing with. The kind of people we know.

POWER Sure. But I'll tell you. Although I've only had a small dose of it, this ... personality cult or whatever it is, I have already had enough. And no matter how hard I try [*shouting*] I just can't get impressed!

NORMAN Lower your voice, man. Where do you think you are?

SAM A beer hall?

POWER Shit, tell me what happened to her estate or I'll have you on welfare by tomorrow afternoon.

SAM You demented pig. You son of a bitching shit-faced – [*And he charges* POWER. POWER *stands. Backs off. Genuinely alarmed. But* NORMAN *gets in the way.* SAM *stops.*]

NORMAN No, Samuel. Remember Father. Never show your contempt. Always mix well. Smile on the outside. But in the back room show no mercy. Our time will come.

SAM [*nods*]. My sincerest apologies, Mr. Power. No harm intended.

NORMAN Yes. Now as for your inquiry into our late client's estate. As you know she was an active supporter of all things cultural. A spontaneous woman, she merely withdrew funds as she went along and passed the cash over to various artists and art organizations. Ergo – and let me repeat that – ergo, when she passed on she left an estate which on paper was twice as much as in actuality. Satisfied?

POWER No. What happened to her copper mine?

NORMAN Nothing.

SAM It never turned into anything.

NORMAN Not unusual if you know anything about mine exploration.

POWER [*Produces a little notebook. Holds it up.*] Homework. [*Reading.*] Grand Divers Copper. Defunct. But there might be some credence to the rumour that it was one of the largest finds on the continent. And what's more that the copper is now being mined in a clandestine operation run by illegal immigrants.

SAM   Stupid rumours.

POWER   But rumours seem to be what makes the world run these days.

NORMAN   True. Why, we even hear them about you, Mr. Power. [NORMAN *produces his own notebook.* SAM *takes his cue from* NORMAN *then does the same.*] The affair you're having with a certain cabinet minister's sister.

SAM   Not to mention what we hear goes on between the brother and sister themselves.

POWER   How do you know these things?

NORMAN   We know just about everything, Mr. Power.

SAM   Annoying, isn't it?

POWER   Gossip.

NORMAN   You don't like gossip. Well, neither do we. And if you care about this minister's sister, and want to spare her a great deal of embarrassment, perhaps you should forget about our business matters and stick to your assignment.

SAM   Which is to solve one simple murder.

POWER   [*Looks at* SAM. *Pause.*] All right. Who would stand to gain the most by Jane Nelson's death?

BOTH   [SAM *and* NORMAN]. Her sister.

POWER   She doesn't seem like the type who is interested in money.

SAM   But money can fulfill dreams.

NORMAN   Even bizarre outrageous dreams about a new world.

SAM   Oh yes, we could tell you stories about her, Mr. Power.

NORMAN   If we didn't abhor gossip so much.

SAM   Yes, if we didn't abhor gossip we could tell you about the Amframs.

POWER   The what?

NORMAN   Samuel.

SAM   Sorry, Mr. Power, you'll just have to find out for yourself.

POWER   Okay. What about Pedro Puchinsky?

NORMAN   He's not a murderer.

SAM   But he is active in other areas. He used to be Jane's lover, but now he has a mystery lady that he keeps hidden for some reason. And everyone is dying to find out who she is.

NORMAN   It's a game. It's terrific fun. The more outrageous the guess, the closer you're supposed to be.

SAM   It could be Brigot Nelson.

NORMAN   Oh God.

Stephen Markle (PETER BELLUM), Maury Chaykin (SAM LEWIS)
and David Bolt (T.M. POWER).

BOTH   That's disgusting.

NORMAN   I think it's the ghost of Phyllis Lazer.

SAM   I think it's Susan Long.

NORMAN   That blonde call girl?

SAM   The one with the three hundred dollar minimum.

NORMAN   You know it could be her. She disappears for long periods of time.

SAM   They say she works half a year in Europe.

POWER   Were all those people at the gallery the night of the murder?

NORMAN   Yes.

POWER   Anybody else?

SAM   No. Just Brigot's houseboy, Allan.

NORMAN   A young actor.

SAM   How could he be an actor? He has a speech impediment.

NORMAN   No. You're thinking of someone else.

SAM   Who? [NORMAN *whispers in* SAM's *ear. They both laugh.*]

POWER   Sorry to interrupt, boys. But could you give me Pedro Puchinsky's phone number?

NORMAN   In the telephone directory.

SAM   With the telephone.

BOTH   [*pointing*]. In there.

POWER   [*Starts off. Stops.*] Pedro Puchinsky. What kind of name is that, anyway?

NORMAN   Spanish-Hungarian.

POWER   Really. He must have a wonderful sense of oppression. [NORMAN *laughs.* POWER *goes off to use the telephone.*]

SAM   I didn't get that.

NORMAN   Neither did I.

SAM   Then why did you laugh?

NORMAN   The man obviously thinks he's witty. He'll be a lot easier to deal with if we don't shatter any illusions.

SAM   How are we doing so far?

NORMAN   [*shrugs*]. Listen, do you think we acted silly enough?

SAM   It's hard to say.

NORMAN   I mean do you think we acted silly enough to make him leave us alone.

SAM   Well if I can be honest.

NORMAN   Well if you wish.

SAM   Well I think I was acting silly enough but you were acting too silly.

41

NORMAN	Really. Why did you mention the Amframs?
SAM	I was told to.
NORMAN	I think it was a mistake. A silly, silly mistake.
SAM	You should talk. You mentioned Phyllis Lazer.
NORMAN	In that case maybe it's good that you mentioned the Amframs. It might confuse him.
SAM	Sometimes I get confused myself.
NORMAN	Well that's an understatement. What was all that demented pig business. You actually attacked the man.
SAM	He made me angry.
NORMAN	You made a fool of yourself. Lawyers don't go around attacking people.
SAM	And lawyers don't go around saying 'Ergo, let me repeat that, ergo'. That's the silliest thing I've ever heard. No one says ergo. No one. I've never been so embarrassed in my life!
NORMAN	You were just nervous.
SAM	Why do you say that?
NORMAN	You looked nervous. You looked very nervous.
SAM	Don't tell me I looked very nervous. You looked very nervous. Very, very nervous.
NORMAN	Oh shut up.
SAM	You shut up.
NORMAN	I mean it.
SAM	I mean it myself.
BOTH	Shut up! [*They grab each other by the throat. Blackout in this area. Lights up on the adjacent area where* MARGARET *and* ANNA *are having a heated discussion.*]
ANNA	You are so.
MARGARET	I am not.
ANNA	I've seen pictures of you with your brother a hundred times.
MARGARET	I look like her. We're the same height. We share certain physical traits. The odd mannerism. Coincidence.
ANNA	I get it. You're having an affair. Why hide it? You're not married. Who is it? One of those guys in there. Can't be Norman or Sam. You're too old. I'm almost too old for them. No. It must be Power.
MARGARET	We're just friends.
ANNA	Sure.
MARGARET	It's the truth.

ANNA Well, in that case, give him this message for me. Tell him I saw Pedro Puchinsky hanging around the champagne the night old lady Nelson was poisoned.

MARGARET The artist?

ANNA Right. And another thing. After Power left our rehearsal hall the other day Peter Bellum got on the phone to Brigot Nelson and about an hour later a chauffeur arrived to pick him up.

MARGARET Pedro Puchinsky, champagne. Peter Bellum, telephone. Brigot Nelson, chauffeur. Anything else?

ANNA Yeah. A lot. But most of it's too hot to pass on without double-checking the facts. A girl could get burned, if you know what I mean.

MARGARET I haven't the slightest idea what you mean.

ANNA Never mind. Tell Power I'll get in touch. Listen, do you think you can pay me for what I've already told you? He said he'd pay me for information.

MARGARET How much is it worth?

ANNA Fifty? [MARGARET *reaches into her purse.*] I've heard lots of stories about you. You're mentally ill, right?

MARGARET Where did you hear that?

ANNA At parties. I go to lots of parties.

MARGARET [*hands her some money*]. Fifty.

ANNA Thanks. Well, are you or aren't you?

MARGARET What?

ANNA Mentally ill?

MARGARET I don't know.

ANNA Well if I were you I'd look into it. It could be serious. Don't take any chances. Look what happened to Phyllis Lazer.

MARGARET Who is she?

ANNA She was Bitch Nelson's personal secretary. Everyone told her she was going insane but she wouldn't believe them. Her behaviour became stranger and stranger and stranger. And finally, she actually got mixed up with a politician. They found her with her head in a toilet in a dingy motel. Overdose. Say, wasn't it your brother who she got mixed up with?

MARGARET No!

ANNA Well I guess you'd know. Sorry about that. I hear so many stories it's hard to keep all the names straight.

MARGARET You should try. People can get hurt.

ANNA	You're telling me. Look at Phyllis Lazer. Well thanks for the money. See you around. Bye. [*She leaves.* MARGARET *closes her eyes.* POWER *comes on.*]
POWER	What was Anna talking to you about?
MARGARET	Pedro Puchinsky. She saw him hanging around the champagne just before Jane Nelson was poisoned. I told you didn't I? Pedro Puchinsky is the prime suspect.
POWER	The Lewis brothers say Brigot Nelson.
MARGARET	Jane's sister?
POWER	You know her?
MARGARET	Only by reputation. A brilliant poet.
POWER	You're familiar with her work?
MARGARET	No. Only her reputation.
POWER	Ever heard of a call girl named Susan Long?
MARGARET	No.
POWER	How about Phyllis Lazer?
MARGARET	No. Why?
POWER	Names the Lewis brothers dropped.
MARGARET	They're just trying to lead you away from Pedro. They're his patrons. Don't trust them.
POWER	I don't trust any of these people.
MARGARET	Did you ask them about Jane Nelson's estate?
POWER	I decided to drop that line of questioning.
MARGARET	The smart thing to do.
POWER	Maybe. [*Pause.*] Margaret?
MARGARET	Yes?
POWER	About you and Paul. No. About you and me.
MARGARET	You mean our relationship?
POWER	Is that what it is. Then why don't we have sex? I mean it's been three years and the farthest you've let me go is to talk about it.
MARGARET	You're too pushy, Tyrone. You know I already have an emotional commitment. If you'd only relax and spend some time with me and let me tell you all my problems and be honest and admit that you love me as much as I love Paul then –
POWER	Enough. Goodbye. [*Starts off.*]
MARGARET	Where are you going?
POWER	To work.
MARGARET	Do you want me to come with you?
POWER	No.

MARGARET	You're lying, aren't you?
POWER	No I'm not. [*Leaves.*]
MARGARET	Oh yes you are. I can tell when you're lying, Mr. Power. It's the only time you look sincere. [*He comes back on.*]
POWER	You're right. [*He takes her hand. They leave.*]
	BACKOUT

Scene Seven

POWER*'s office.* BAXTER *is gagged and tied to a chair. A masked man is in the process of ransacking the place. Papers are already strewn all over. In the distance we hear voices. Very loud.* POWER *and* MARGARET *are arguing. Gradually getting closer.*

POWER	I'm busy. If you don't like it, go home. You make too many demands.
MARGARET	You promised me we'd spend some time alone together, Tyrone. In a relationship a person has the right to make certain demands.
POWER	We don't have a relationship.
MARGARET	Yes we do! Just because we don't go to bed together doesn't mean we don't have a relationship.
POWER	It does to me!
MARGARET	Just because I don't love you doesn't mean that you can't love me.
POWER	They call that unrequited love, Margaret. It's a disease. People wither away from it. They move into rooming houses and die, staring at the little triangles on the linoleum floors.
MARGARET	Romantic garbage.
POWER	Easy for you. You've been in love since the first time you and Paul had a bath together.
MARGARET	That's not fair.
POWER	Get out of my life. [*They appear.*]
MARGARET	I can't. I need someone to talk to about my tension. [*The masked man and* BAXTER *have been staring in their direction for some time.* POWER *and* MARGARET *stop. The*

masked man points a gun at them. Gestures for them to raise their hands and move to a corner. They obey. The masked man continues his search.]

MARGARET What's he doing?

POWER What the hell does he look like he's doing? Don't be stupid.

MARGARET Don't be rude. I never insult *you*.

POWER What do you think you do to me every time you tell me another little story about you and your brother?

MARGARET I'm just trying to get it straight in my head. You have no compassion.

POWER I had it once. You dissolved it.

MARGARET Excuses! You've been like this for years. All you do is reject. Never give. Just reject. Even in your work. You never offer alternatives. You just reject everything.

POWER That's my function.

MARGARET That's not a function! [BAXTER *is groaning. Moving violently around.*]

POWER Shut up, Baxter. That's what you get for hanging around my office. [BAXTER *throws him a strange look. Becomes silent. The masked man, bewildered by their behaviour, has stopped his search and is just standing there watching them. His gun more or less pointing in their direction. To masked man.*] Listen. Do me a favour? Search all you want. Take anything that catches your fancy. But don't point that gun at me. Thanks very much.

MARGARET You're so clinical. The man is standing there with a gun. He could be a raving psychopath for all you know. And you talk to him like you're ordering coffee from your messenger boy.

POWER He's just doing his job. I know a raving psychopath when I see one. You're a raving psychopath.

MARGARET But why don't you ever look on the bright side.

POWER Get out of my life.

MARGARET Admit you love me.

POWER I love you.

MARGARET Admit you care about me.

POWER I care about you.

MARGARET I can't tell you how happy that makes me feel.

POWER Try. [*She pulls his face in, kisses him. They embrace. A long kiss.* BAXTER *and the masked man look at them. Look at each other.* BAXTER *starts to move around and groan again. Masked man lowers his gun. Continues his search.* BRIGOT NELSON *comes in. She is wearing a tweed suit.*]

BRIGOT Have you found it? [*Masked man mumbles something.*] Oh take off that ridiculous mask. This isn't theatre. It's crime. [*Masked man takes off mask. It is* ALLAN *the actor, houseboy.*]

ALLAN I didn't want to be identified.

BRIGOT Face like yours? Small chance. You've been working for me for two years and I can barely remember what you look like from day to day. Now have you found it?

ALLAN No.

BRIGOT Then keep searching. [MARGARET *and* POWER *are looking at each other.*]

POWER Why did you kiss me?

MARGARET To thank you for telling me that you cared.

POWER That's the only reason?

MARGARET Of course.

POWER Goddamnit. [*Gestures wildly. Becomes mobile.*] That's it. That's enough. Everyone out of my office.

BRIGOT Allan?

ALLAN Yes, Miss Nelson.

BRIGOT Kill him.

ALLAN Yes, Miss Nelson. [*He points the gun at* POWER.]

BRIGOT Not him, Allan. We need him to tell us where it is. [*Points to* BAXTER.] Kill that one. [BAXTER*'s eyes widen. He starts to groan and shake his head.* POWER *chuckles. Goes over. Puts an arm on* BAXTER*'s shoulder.*]

POWER Now if you didn't hang around my office, Baxter, this wouldn't be happening to you. They're serious, you know. Whatever it is she's after might not be important to us but is probably a matter of life and death to her. [*To* BRIGOT.] Correct?

BRIGOT Life and death is a bit extreme. If we're going to use a cliché let's just say I want it so bad I can almost taste it.

POWER You see, Baxter? She's gone to all this trouble just because she wants something to eat. [BAXTER *groans.*] Baxter says you should eat shit. [BAXTER *groans louder.*]

BRIGOT Allan.

ALLAN   I'm psyching myself up, Miss Nelson.

BRIGOT   Just think of it as if you're in a play, boy. It's the middle of Act Two. The play is taking a dark twist. You're the protagonist. He's the comic relief. He has to be disposed of.

ALLAN   Oh, what a rogue and peasant slave am I. [*Two hands on the gun.*] Stella! Stella! [BAXTER *whimpers. Closes his eyes.*]

POWER   Hold on. [*Reaches into his breast pocket.*] Here. [*Has produced a rolled-up piece of paper.*]

BRIGOT   Bring it here, Allan. [ALLAN *gets it. Takes it to* BRIGOT. *She examines it.*] Fine. Wait for me in the car. [ALLAN *leaves.*] When you play with me, Mr. Power, you play with one of the world's natural forces. Next time hire an army.

POWER   I intend to.

BRIGOT   Hello Margaret.

MARGARET   Hello Brigot.

BRIGOT   How is your brother?

MARGARET   He's fine. [POWER *looks at them both.*]

BRIGOT   That's nice.

MARGARET   I'm sorry about Jane. I liked her.

BRIGOT   Yes. And I'm sorry about Phyllis Lazer. You and Paul must be very upset. Well, goodnight.

MARGARET   Goodnight. [BRIGOT *starts off. Stops.*]

BRIGOT   [*to* POWER]. You will of course forget everything you read on that document.

POWER   Worried about the Amframs?

BRIGOT   Forget about the Amframs. They're of no concern to you.

POWER   I hear little voices in my head telling me otherwise.

BRIGOT   And where do you suppose your little voices got their information?

POWER   Various sources.

BRIGOT   None of them trustworthy.

POWER   Maybe.

BRIGOT   I'm telling you you're being led astray.

POWER   But the question is by whom.

BRIGOT   Look. Just keep your nose out of my business. Concentrate on solving my sister's murder. And you'll be doing a lot of good.

POWER   I'm not interested in doing good, lady. I'm interested in getting at the truth.

BRIGOT   Don't give me that hysterical soap-box gibberish. We live

in a complex age. Truth is a relative commodity beyond
your grasp. Come to grips with your limitations, man.
Solve one simple murder. Take the applause. And retire!
[*She leaves.* MARGARET *is untying* BAXTER's *gag.*]

BAXTER Goddamn you, Power. You almost got me killed.

POWER Yeah. Almost.

BAXTER What's this all about anyway. What was on that paper?

POWER A political manifesto written in blank verse outlining
plans for a new world.

BAXTER Go to hell. I'm going after those people. They can't get
away with this. [*Runs off.*]

POWER How well do you know Brigot Nelson, Margaret?

MARGARET Hardly at all.

POWER Why didn't you mention it?

MARGARET When?

POWER When we were breaking into her house.

MARGARET I didn't know it was her house, Tyrone. I didn't even know
we were breaking into it. I just thought we were visiting
someone. Until you smashed that window.

POWER What about Phyllis Lazer?

MARGARET What about her?

POWER Back at the Lewis brothers' house you said you'd never
heard of her.

MARGARET I was confused.

POWER But you do know her.

MARGARET Did. She's dead.

POWER And how did she die?

MARGARET An accident of some kind, I think.

POWER Is that what Paul told you?

MARGARET What's Paul got to do with it?

POWER Brigot Nelson said *Paul* and you must be very upset.

MARGARET Drop it, Tyrone.

POWER Not on your life.

MARGARET Well, it *is* my life and I'm warning you. There's enough
tension in it already!

BAXTER [*runs back on*]. They got away. Power, I'm warning you. I
want to know what all this is about. [POWER *takes a gun out
of his coat pocket.*]

MARGARET Tyrone?

BAXTER What's that for?

POWER Protection. Lots of people are 'warning' me, you see. I could get hurt. [*Puts the gun in the desk drawer.* BAXTER *and* MARGARET *look at each other. They look at* POWER. POWER *smiles.*] Now get out of my office. Both of you. [*They look at him. Each other. Slowly leave.* POWER *takes off his jacket. His shoes. Sits on the desk. Closes his eyes. Opens his eyes. Stands. Paces a while. Sits on the edge of the desk. Stares off.*] This is what we have so far. Jane Nelson a.k.a. 'that Bitch' who may or may not have been bisexual, and who cares, was murdered by someone at a gallery showing by an artist who was possibly her jilted lover, and so what, leaving behind an immense estate to be fudged by a couple of lawyers who want me to think they're the silliest bastards on the face of the earth. But fudged for what purpose? What was Norman Lewis doing in Argentina? Something to do with the Amframs? If so why would Sam Lewis have mentioned them. What does Brigot Nelson really intend to do. Is that document what it appears to be? Or is it a plant to throw me off? Off what? Pedro Puchinsky, God I hate that name, doesn't answer his door or his phone. Is Susan Long his mystery lady and what's so bizarre about that? Unless she killed Jane Nelson. And if so why? Love triangle? If that's all, the police would have figured it out. But if Nelson's murder is tied to something more then maybe Susan Long and Pedro Puchinsky are as well. [*Pause.*] Phyllis Lazer. What happened to Phyllis Lazer? [*Reaches inside his desk for the telephone directory. Flips through the pages. Finds his page.*] Lazer. Lazer Phyllis. Lazer Sylvia. Sylvia. Might be a relative. [*Dials the phone.*] I wish I was better at this. I feel sort of vulnerable. Hello. Sylvia Lazer? Are you related to the late Phyllis Lazer? Yes, well I just wanted to say how sorry I am about your sister. My name? Name is ... Townsend. I'm an ... insurance investigator. [*Smiles.*]

BLACKOUT

Scene Eight

Later. POWER'*s office.* POWER, *looking very tired, is going
through some papers on his desk. Making notes. Stuffing
envelopes, addressing them. Radio is on. A Beethoven
sonata. Goes on like this for a while. Finally* BAXTER *comes
in. Stands there for a moment before speaking.*

BAXTER Why don't you get some sleep?

POWER Things to do.

BAXTER I've got a letter here for you. First class from Argentina, of
all places. Can I have the stamp?

POWER [*takes letter*]. Sure.

BAXTER The guy it's from. This A.P. Tucker. Who is he?

POWER An ex-journalist. Now runs a brothel in Buenos Aires.
Knows everything that goes on down there.

BAXTER You're still working on the Jane Nelson murder, aren't
you?

POWER That and more. Much more.

BAXTER What?

POWER Later, Baxter.

BAXTER Well, I won't push. That's what my father used to say.
Never push a reporter when he's on the job. Let him find
his own rhythms.

POWER Must have been one of his rare moments of clarity.

BAXTER Try to be respectful of my father.

POWER Sure. [*They just look at each other.*]

BAXTER Anything I can do to help?

POWER Hire a detective. Find me Pedro Puchinsky. He's missing.

BAXTER I'll get right on it. [*Turns.*]

POWER Oh by the way, I received two anonymous calls this
evening.

BAXTER More threats?

POWER One of them. The other offered information.

BAXTER Maybe someone's trying to help you.

POWER Or confuse me. I have a feeling I'm being used.

BAXTER What makes you say that?

POWER Just a feeling.

BAXTER Look, Power. I'm sorry if this thing has caused you – I mean here you are with a gun in your desk drawer – and all that trouble with Margaret and her brother whatever that is –

POWER Did you feed my dog?

BAXTER I took Margaret to your apartment. She was really upset about –

POWER Did you feed my dog?

BAXTER I've never seen Margaret like that. She was shaking and –

POWER Did you feed my dog?

BAXTER Yes I fed your goddamn dog. And do you want to know something. That dog's a disgrace. He smells. His fur is matted. And he shits all over the place. You're both a disgrace. There's nothing but shit all over your apartment. Why don't you ever pick it up, Power? [*No response.* BAXTER *shakes his head. Leaves.*]

POWER It's his shit. Why should I pick it up? [*He takes a couple of reference books from a drawer in his desk. Also an atlas. Opens it. Continues making notes while looking through all these books. A stunning lady in a blonde wig, a sexy dress and sunglasses comes into the office. It is obviously* MARGARET.]

SUSAN They tell me you've been looking for me. [POWER *looks up.*] I'm Susan Long.

POWER Oh my God. [*Puts his head down on the desk.*]

SUSAN Well, I've gotten a lot of different reactions from men in my time. What is it? Something wrong with the way I look? [POWER *lifts his head.*]

POWER You always look good.

SUSAN What?

POWER Forget it! [*Pours himself a drink.*]

SUSAN Well you don't have to get testy. I've come here to help you. [POWER *stares at her for a moment.*]

POWER Yeah? How?

SUSAN I know who killed Jane Nelson.

POWER Sit down.

SUSAN Can I have a drink? [POWER *takes out another glass. Pours two drinks. A toast.*] Happy Friday.

Scene Eight

POWER It's Monday.

SUSAN Another lost weekend. Good thing I'm in my prime.

POWER All right. Who killed Jane Nelson?

SUSAN Pedro Puchinsky.

POWER Where is he?

SUSAN The last I heard, he was planning to paint the expressway orange. Opus Eight-five, he called it.

POWER He's missing.

SUSAN Well he has a lot of orange paint.

POWER It's very interesting that you should be pointing the finger at Pedro.

SUSAN Why?

POWER You were his lover, weren't you?

SUSAN Listen, I'm a working girl.

POWER Jesus Christ!

SUSAN Are you some kind of moralist?

POWER No.

SUSAN Then watch your attitude.

POWER Let's talk about Susan Long.

SUSAN Well if we're going to get heavy I might as well take off my coat. [*She does.*] By the way, what do you think of my coat?

POWER It's incredible.

SUSAN It cost five thousand dollars.

POWER That's a lot of money.

SUSAN To you that's a lot of money. A friend bought it for me. Five thousand means nothing to him. Therefore the coat means nothing to me. It's yours.

POWER I don't want it.

SUSAN Too proud to take a little gift? You got hang-ups about things like that?

POWER All right, I'll take the bloody coat! [*He does. Hangs it up.*]

SUSAN They told me you were a miserable son of a bitch.

POWER Who sent you here.

SUSAN Discretion, sweetheart. In my business it's a big thing.

POWER Your business? Oh for Christ's sake!

SUSAN Now I told you to watch your attitude. I like my work. I like the freedom it gives me. I like myself. Okay?

POWER I hear you disappear for about six months every year. Where do you go?

SUSAN Europe. I have several apartments in Europe.

POWER   You've never been to Europe. But you have been to Argentina.

SUSAN   Well, I'm going to have a word with my travel agent first thing in the morning. One of us is very confused.

POWER   The last time you were there for three months.

SUSAN   I'm never anywhere for three months. I get bored.

POWER   You had plenty to do. And lots of company. Brigot Nelson. The Lewis brothers.

SUSAN   The Lewis brothers. They're entertainers, aren't they?

POWER   Yeah. Song and dance team.

SUSAN   Where did you get all this information about me?

POWER   I have a friend in Buenos Aires.

SUSAN   Wow.

POWER   Tell me all you know about the Amframs.

SUSAN   The what?

POWER   Amframs. Like in Amframica for the Amframs.

SUSAN   Never heard of any of those things. But if I were you I'd forget about them.

POWER   Why?

SUSAN   It might lead you into areas that are most unpleasant.

POWER   It already has. Now who sent you here?

SUSAN   No one. I just thought you could use my help.

POWER   You're the one who needs help. [*He grabs her.*] Don't you know who you are? Don't you know what they're making you do?

SUSAN   I get it, you want to play identity games. [*Puts her arm around him.*] I can be whoever you want. I can be a movie star. I can be your mother. [*Kisses him.*] Do you have any favourites?

POWER   I don't have three hundred dollars, Susan.

SUSAN   There are other ways to pay.

POWER   How?

SUSAN   Forget about the Amframs. Forget about Jane Nelson's copper mine. Just solve one simple murder.

POWER   That's enough. [*Breaks away.*] That's too much. Here, this is for you.

SUSAN   What is it?

POWER   An invitation to a party I'm giving for all your 'friends'. You like parties, I suppose.

SUSAN   Sure. But I'm a very busy girl.

POWER   Read it. You'll be there.

SUSAN   Don't set your poor little heart on it, okay?

POWER   Get out of here. I've got some scores to settle.

SUSAN   My coat. [POWER *turns to get coat.*]

POWER   Indian giver. [SUSAN *pulls the gun from* POWER's *drawer.*
Points it at him. POWER *turns. They both look at the gun.*
POWER *takes it from her. Puts the coat over her shoulder.*
She bows her head. Leaves. POWER *slowly lifts the gun.*
Points at the rose in the typewriter. Empties the gun.
Disintegrating the rose.]
BLACKOUT

Scene Nine

A large room. A long lavishly set table. It is a formal affair.
Everyone should be dressed accordingly. BAXTER, *dressed*
in a waiter's uniform, is pouring himself a drink. He is
already a bit drunk. PETER BELLUM *comes on.*

BELLUM   I'm early.

BAXTER   Yes you are.

BELLUM   Well, look at this then. Very impressive indeed. Should be
interesting. No better theatre than when one has a
physical activity to watch. And eating is one of the best.

BAXTER   This is a dinner party.

BELLUM   It's theatre. People are coming here to perform. Some of
them may even be good at it. Lies will be told. Accusations
will be thrown around the room without remorse. My life
is in danger.

BAXTER   What makes you say that?

BELLUM   Are you trying to imply that I'm paranoid?

BAXTER   What makes you say that?

BELLUM   Here's one hundred dollars.

BAXTER   What's it for?

BELLUM   I need a friend.

BAXTER   What makes you think I can be trusted?

BELLUM   I'm desperate.

55

BAXTER   I'll think about it.

BELLUM   Better than nothing. Now where will Mr. Power be sitting? [BAXTER *points to a chair.*] Thank you. Where's the kitchen? [BAXTER *points.*] Thank you. Say nothing. I'll be back. When we meet again be blasé. [*He goes into the kitchen.* MARGARET *and* POWER *come on.* POWER *is wearing a dinner jacket.* MARGARET *is still wearing the trenchcoat. During the exchange* BAXTER *will be trying in vain to get* POWER*'s attention.*]

MARGARET   Why won't you tell me what you're up to?

POWER   It's a surprise.

MARGARET   I have a terrible feeling you're going to do something to hurt me. [POWER *grabs a pickle from the table. Eats it.*]

POWER   Whatever happens. Try to remember that I have your best interests at heart.

MARGARET   Then you really are going to hurt me.

POWER   Trust me.

MARGARET   Why should I?

POWER   Because I trusted you [*Starts off.*]

MARGARET   Where are you going now?

POWER   Washroom. To straighten my tie. [*He leaves.*]

MARGARET   [*following him*]. I couldn't sleep at all last night. [*Leaves.*]

BAXTER   Neither could I. [ALLAN *comes in. Cases the place. Leaves.* ALLAN *returns. Followed by* BRIGOT NELSON. *She points to a chair at the head of the table. He pulls it out. She sits.*]

BRIGOT   They're late.

BAXTER   You're early.

BRIGOT   I should have had you killed. Judging from your new position I would have been doing you a favour. Get me a glass of sherry. [*There is a small liquor table behind* BAXTER. *He nods. Turns. Looks for the sherry.* POWER *comes on. Tie still not right. Stops at* BAXTER*'s side.*]

POWER   She's early. Tell her to leave.

BAXTER   Tell her yourself!

POWER   What's wrong with you?

BAXTER   Nothing. Where's Margaret?

POWER   Washroom. Crying. Fix my tie. [BAXTER *proceeds to fix* POWER*'s tie.*]

BAXTER   When are you going to tell me what this is all about?

POWER   I'm not. I'm going to let you find out all by yourself. That's what investigative journalism is about.

BAXTER   I hate to think that you've gone to all this trouble just to make me feel like an asshole. [*Points to the uniform.*]

POWER   Relax. It suits you.

ANNA   [*Comes in. Dressed in a maid's uniform. Carrying a floral arrangement.*] Hi, Power. How come I'm supposed to wear this uniform?

POWER   Because it wouldn't fit Baxter. [*He smiles.*] [*She goes back into the kitchen.*]

BAXTER   Is she in on it?

POWER   'It'? What's an 'it', Baxter?

BAXTER   I don't know.

POWER   Well let me know when you do. Meanwhile get me a vodka martini. One ice cube. And bring it to the table. [*Takes a chair next to* BRIGOT.] Good evening, Miss Nelson. You look ravishing. [BRIGOT *reaches over. Grabs him by the collar.*]

BRIGOT   What was all that horse crap you wrote on my invitation, you little puke?

POWER   I know about your sister and her money and Pedro Puchinsky and all the rest of it.

BRIGOT   You're pissing in the air, Power. Watch out for sudden breezes.

MARGARET   [*Comes on.*] Hello. [POWER *and* BRIGOT *smile.* BRIGOT *lets go of his collar. They turn to* MARGARET. *Smile.*]

BRIGOT   Hello, dear.

POWER   Sit down, dear. There. [MARGARET *sits in the chair* POWER *has pointed to.* BAXTER *comes over with two drinks on a tray.*]

BAXTER   Sherry with one ice cube. Vodka martini. [*Puts the drinks down.*]

BRIGOT   Take that back. You don't put ice in sherry. [BAXTER *takes the sherry. Takes the ice out. Puts it in the martini.*] That man is too stupid to be out without parental supervision.

POWER   He's read all your poetry.

BRIGOT   In some scientific laboratories apes read Goethe. It doesn't mean they should be let out of their cages.

BAXTER   Sherry without ice! [*Slams it down in front of her.*]

SAM   [*Comes on.*] Good evening, Mr. Power. Good evening, Brigot. Allan. Good evening.

MARGARET   Margaret.

SAM   Good evening. [*To* POWER.] Where do I sit? [POWER *points to a chair.* SAM *sits in it.*]

POWER	Where's your brother?
SAM	He sends his apologies.
POWER	How thoughtful. [BAXTER *is now drunk for sure and getting drunker as he keeps taking quick drinks every time he passes the liquor table.*]
SAM	[*snapping his fingers*]. Boy! Boy!
BAXTER	Whatya want?!
SAM	Your waiter has no manners.
POWER	Into the kitchen with you, Baxter. You're not fit to be with civilized people.
SAM	But first he should bring me a Manhattan.
BAXTER	I don't know how to make a Manhattan.
POWER	Improvise.
SAM	I'd rather he didn't. [*Gets up.*] I'll make it myself.
BAXTER	You have true humility. I can hardly wait to tell the kitchen help. They say you're just a nouveau riche punk.
SAM	Was that meant to be ironic, Mr. Power?
POWER	Tyrone. Call me Tyrone. I want you all to think of me as one of the gang. Everyone, please call me Tyrone. [*They all look at him oddly.*]
BAXTER	Can I speak to you a moment, Tyrone?
POWER	Except you.
BAXTER	[*Recovers quickly. To* POWER *confidentially.*] I've got something very important to tell you.
POWER	What is it? [PETER BELLUM *comes in.*]
BAXTER	Later.
POWER	Ah, Peter. Glad you could make it.
BELLUM	I never miss a spectacle. [*He sits.* BAXTER *staggers over to* BELLUM. *Puts the hundred dollars in his hand.*] Why are you doing this?
BAXTER	You were right. Your life isn't worth a sou. [BAXTER *giggles. Goes back into the kitchen.*]
BELLUM	Oh Tyrone. Come here for a moment, will you?
POWER	Will you excuse me, Miss Nelson? [BRIGOT *just waves him away.* POWER *stands. Makes his way towards* BELLUM. *Stops behind* MARGARET. *Puts a hand on her shoulder.*]
POWER	Enjoying yourself, Margaret?
MARGARET	No.
POWER	Fibber. [*She looks at him oddly. But he has already moved on to* BELLUM. *Sits next to him.*]

BELLUM [*whispering*]. I think you've made a mistake.

POWER [*whispering*]. What do you mean? [*And they proceed in whispers.*]

BELLUM You sent me the wrong invitation. All that talk about plots and conspiracy. I told you I'm not one of them. I didn't understand a word of what you were talking about.

POWER Then maybe you'll understan this. [*Takes and 8 x 10 glossy from inside his coat. Hands it to him.* BELLUM *looks at it. Pales. Starts to stand.* POWER *puts a hand on his shoulder. Pushes him down.*] You can't leave.

BELLUM Why not?

POWER Police are outside.

BELLUM [*at a normal level*]. Police?

POWER Shush. It's a secret.

BELLUM Why are you doing this to me?

POWER You tried to make a fool out of me. I don't like that.

BELLUM No, you don't understand. Sam forced me to do it. [SAM *looks at* BELLUM. BELLUM *looks at* SAM.] I mean Brigot forced me to do it. [BRIGOT *looks at* BELLUM. BELLUM *looks at* BRIGOT.] Actually, that's not right. It was Anna. Anna forced me to do it. [ANNA *and* BAXTER *have come on carrying trays.* ANNA *goes right to* BELLUM.]

ANNA Forced you to do what, Mr. Bellum?

BELLUM [*startled*]. Oh dear. Power you have to protect me. [BRIGOT *stands.* SAM *stands.* ANNA *turns toward* BELLUM.] Oh stop it. Stop it. Everyone stop it.

POWER Yes. Everyone stop it and sit down. Dinner is about to be served. [BRIGOT *and* SAM *sit.* POWER *pats* BELLUM *on the head. Leaves him.* BELLUM *is looking fearfully at them all.* POWER *takes his seat. There are three empty chairs around the table.* BAXTER *leans over to him.*]

BAXTER Where are the rest of them?

POWER Don't worry. Serve the soup.

BAXTER Listen, I just remembered that important thing I wanted to tell you. [*Smiles.*] Someone is going to try to kill you.

POWER Serve the soup. [BAXTER *and* ANNA *serve the soup. Placing bowls in front of the empty chairs as well.* POWER *eats heartily.* SAM *eats a bit, looks around, eats a bit, etc.* BELLUM *just stares at his soup and the photo.* BRIGOT *and* ALLAN *taste the soup. He nods. She tastes it herself. Makes a face of disgust. Hands it to* ALLAN *who eats the rest.* MARGARET *eats slowly. Looking only at* POWER.] Good soup, eh?

BRIGOT I've never been very fond of cream of spinach.

POWER Compliments to the chef, Baxter.

BAXTER He'll be pleased as punch.

SAM Don't I know you from somewhere?

MARGARET No.

POWER How do you like your soup, Sam?

SAM I'm not much of a soup eater, Tyrone.

POWER Was Norman? [*A sudden silence punctuated by a knife dropping.*]

SAM What do you mean 'was'?

POWER Slip of the tongue, Sam. Peter, you're not touching yours. Something wrong?

BELLUM There's too much tension in the room.

POWER Shut up! [BRIGOT *is tapping the table with her knife.*] Did you want to say something, Miss Nelson.

BRIGOT I'm trying to control myself.

POWER Very interesting grip you have on that knife.

BRIGOT I'm trying very, very hard.

POWER Good. [*Picks up bowl. Drinks the rest of his soup.*] Finished. [*Pounds the table.*] Main course, Baxter. [BAXTER *starts off.*] No, no, Baxter. First you clear off the soup dishes. Then you serve the main course.

SAM Are you sure I don't know you from somewhere?

MARGARET I told you no!

POWER Right, Sam?

SAM I don't know.

POWER Too bad Norman isn't here. He'd know. Do you know, Peter? [BAXTER *and* ANNA *are picking up the soup dishes.* BELLUM *stands.*]

BELLUM I can't take it any more!

POWER Sit down! [*They all look at* BELLUM. *He sits.* BAXTER *leans over to* POWER.]

BAXTER Stop messing around, Power. And get to the point for Christ's sake.

POWER You're plastered.

BAXTER So what?

POWER If I were you I'd sober up. Somebody might try to kill you.

BAXTER	Who?
POWER	Me. [BAXTER *grabs* ANNA. *They go into the kitchen.*] Listen, now, I don't want you all to get your hopes up but I passed through the kitchen earlier and I think the main course is really going to be something super.
MARGARET	Tyrone, may I speak to you in private.
POWER	No.
MARGARET	Then I think I'll leave. [*She leaves.* ANNA *and* BAXTER *come on carrying trays. Begin to serve the main course.*]
POWER	Son of a bitch. What did I tell you. Chicken champagne creole. Do you realize that this dish is almost a legend in its own time. Let your hair down guys. And eat like pigs. [MARGARET *comes back on.*]
MARGARET	Those people out there. Photographers. Gossip columnists. Reporters. What are they doing here? [POWER *shrugs.* ALLAN *is eating* BRIGOT's *creole.* BRIGOT *stands suddenly.*]
BRIGOT	This is the five minute warning. Double-check your plans and study your escape routes. Brigot Nelson is giving notice. [BAXTER *staggers over to her.*]
BAXTER	I'm not afraid of you.
BRIGOT	You should be. [*Slaps him.*]
POWER	Now there's a lady who studies her subtext.
BRIGOT	Do it, Allan.
ALLAN	I'm doing it, Miss Nelson. [ALLAN *pulls a gun. Lets it rest against his chest.*]
BRIGOT	Five minutes, Mr. Power. Pick a god. Any god. And put your life in his hands.
POWER	That's a threat, isn't it? Never mind, it's good advice. Everyone pick a god. Then eat. Peter. Eat!
BELLUM	Please don't hurt me.
ALL	Eat! [BELLUM *takes a mouthful. Passes out. His face in the chicken creole.* POWER *stands. Goes to* BELLUM's *side.*]
POWER	Now, what caused that? The food? A sudden recurrence of a childhood trauma? Or this? [*He picks up the photo.*] An 8 x 10 glossy of Mr. Bellum with added touches by yours truly. [*Hands it to* SAM.] Recognize that man, Sam?
SAM	No.
POWER	Odd.

61

Meg Hogarth (BRIGOT NELSON), Jim Henshaw (BAXTER)
and David Bolt (T.M. POWER).

BAXTER   Who killed Jane Nelson?!

POWER   Not yet. First. Who killed Norman Lewis?

SAM   What the hell are you talking about.

POWER   He's been dead for six months. [*Takes the photo. Passes it around.*] Peter Bellum director was once Peter Bellum actor. A bit of make-up. And he becomes Norman Lewis. Definitely not well enough for anyone who knew Norman but enough to pass for my benefit. So much has been done for my benefit. Too much.

SAM   Well, that's your problem, Mr. Power. I'm leaving.

POWER   It's your problem too. [*Grabs him.*]

SAM   Get out of my way.

POWER   I'm not finished yet. Now sit down before [*gestures to* BAXTER] he gets tough. [SAM *sits.*] Now where were we?

BAXTER   Who killed Norman Lewis? [SAM *stands.*]

POWER   Not yet. [SAM *sits.*] First. Who killed Phyllis Lazer?

BAXTER   Who the hell is she?

POWER   Jane Nelson's secretary.

MARGARET   It was suicide, Tyrone.

POWER   No it wasn't.

BAXTER   Then who killed her?

POWER   No I've changed my mind. Let's start with Pedro Puchinsky. Go ahead, Baxter.

BAXTER   All right. Who killed Pedro Puchinsky?

POWER   No one. The man does not exist.

BAXTER   Whatya mean he doesn't exist. He was at the art gallery the night of the murder ... wasn't he?

POWER   Someone was impersonating him. The name Puchinsky is actually a code name for some strange going-on in Argentina of all places.

BRIGOT   [*stands*]. That Argentina does not exist either. It is a black hole on the face of the world. In its bleak and soggy jungles lie the people of the future. We call these people Amframs. We call their country Amframica. [*She sits.*]

POWER   Bizarre you say? Well, about five years ago Miss Nelson discovered a new race of people in the jungles of Argentina. An untouched civilization. People as innocent as children. Brigot Nelson went, she saw and she started having visions.

63

BRIGOT They're a little people with slim hips, bright eyes and lilting sing-song voices. And when they meet the rest of the human race the sun will shine forever. [*Everyone has been making strange incredulous faces during her speech except* POWER.]

POWER A true poet.

BAXTER A dangerous lunatic.

POWER Both. A poet with a lunatic vision. And not enough money to make it real.

BRIGOT Enough. You've been warned. Allan. Kill him. [ALLAN *points the gun at* BAXTER.] Not him Allan. [*Points to* POWER.] Kill him. [ALLAN *walks to* POWER. *Hands him the gun.*]

POWER I bought him, Brigot. He's mine. [*To* ALLAN.] Sit down. You too, Anna. Sit down. Now what was I saying?

BAXTER The money!

POWER Jane Nelson had a copper mine. Convince her that it was nothing, then continue to mine it for your own purposes. A complicated scheme. Lots of financial maneuvering needed. Approach the Lewis brothers. Sam agreed. Norman didn't. Ergo –

BAXTER Kill Norman!

POWER Right.

BAXTER Who, for Christ's sake?

POWER Anna. During a sexual encounter.

ANNA You have no proof. You don't even have a corpse.

POWER But I have a witness. Sam?

SAM I saw nothing.

POWER You're not my witness, Sam. I just wanted to make sure you were still conscious. Allan?

ALLAN She killed Norman Lewis. I saw her. Miss Nelson had sent me over to give the Lewis brothers a message. I heard a commotion in the bedroom. Looked in and saw her stabbing him.

POWER But why would Brigot Nelson have sent her houseboy to witness a murder that she had arranged?

BRIGOT I didn't.

POWER That's right. She didn't. And she didn't want Allan to kill me because I was going to expose her as a murderer, but because I was going to expose her as an idealistic fool.

BRIGOT Oh yes. Here it comes. The disgusting truth.

POWER She needed someone who could use his power to make her Amframs a worldwide issue. She took her idea to a certain cabinet minister. He thought it was dumb, which it is. But when she mentioned her sister's copper mine as a source of revenue the cabinet minister's seedy little brain started working overtime.

MARGARET I have to go to the bathroom.

POWER Later. Now this cabinet minister was in deep financial trouble. A few kickbacks had kicked back. He approached the Lewis brothers. Not directly but through an acquaintance and this acquaintance was the one who, when Norman refused to co-operate, arranged to have him killed.

BAXTER Let me guess.

POWER Phyllis Lazer.

BAXTER I thought so.

POWER Sure you did. Yes. Phyllis Lazer and this cabinet minister were lovers.

MARGARET That's gossip. Evil useless gossip.

POWER It's true, Margaret. Phyllis Lazer was his lover. She'd do anything for him. She's the one who hired Anna to kill Norman. I found that out by talking to Phyllis Lazer's sister Sylvia. She told me that after Phyllis died Anna came by to collect an envelope Phyllis had left for her. The envelope contained two thousand dollars. Why does a woman living on a secretary's salary leave an almost total stranger two thousand dollars?

ANNA She liked me. She thought I had potential.

POWER Not bad. But polish it up a bit and talk it over with your lawyer before you perform it in public. Now where does a secretary like Phyllis Lazer get two thousand dollars in the first place. And that brings us to *her* death.

MARGARET Suicide!

POWER Murder.

MARGARET You have no proof!

POWER But I have a truck load of circumstantial evidence. He was seen with her the night before she was found with her head in that toilet bowl. He gave her that two thousand dollars. I've talked to his accountant. Here's the cancelled cheque. Baxter, can I have five thousand dollars to pay off the accountant?

BAXTER Sure.

MARGARET But why would he have killed her?

POWER She was getting nervous and threatening to confess. So he made one of his famous expedient decisions.

BAXTER Who?!

POWER Her brother, stupid.

MARGARET Circumstantial evidence doesn't convict.

POWER I'll get him, Margaret. If I don't get him as an accomplice in the Norman Lewis, Phyllis Lazer murders, I'll get him on the copper mine scheme. And if I don't get him on that I'll get him sure as hell on those goddamn stinking kickbacks.

MARGARET Please don't.

POWER That man's an insect. He doesn't even do his own killing. He gets his mistress to do it and then he gets his sister to try and cover up.

MARGARET What do you mean?

POWER Later. Now what have we got so far. Pedro Puchinsky does not exist. Argentina does not really exist. The copper mine is not supposed to exist. And Phyllis Lazer and Norman Lewis were forced not to exist. Almost an existentialist's utopia, isn't it?

BRIGOT I've been used.

POWER Me too. And the Amframs are now being used to mine the copper at a pay of two avocados a day, by the way. But Paul and Sam weren't content to use Brigot's dumb but idealistic plan for their own personal gain, they also attempted to blame her for all the other crimes. And that's how they used *me*. Peter Bellum mentioned Argentina. Sam Lewis mentioned the Amframs. Norman Lewis who was really Peter Bellum mentioned Pedro Puchinsky's mystery lady Susan Long figuring it would lead to Brigot's scheme. But Brigot caught on to the fact that she was being set up and tried to protect herself by sending Susan Long to see me. And that's where it all went wrong for everyone.

BAXTER [*stoned-drunk*]. All right! Which one of you bastards killed Susan Long?

POWER Susan Long is alive, Baxter.

BAXTER Well you win some, you lose some.

POWER Not a very good disguise at all, Margaret.

MARGARET I don't know what you mean. But whatever I did, I did for Paul.

POWER Your psychiatrist would say that you were subconsciously trying to have Paul found out. To get him out of your life.

MARGARET Not true. I love him.

POWER Goddamnit, he used you. I talked to your psychiatrist. He told me you hadn't used that Susan Long identity for six months. But Paul persuaded you to get back into it and to go to Brigot to make sure she had no plans to implicate him. What he didn't know was that she was going to send Susan Long to me.

MARGARET [*crying*]. Paul had so much to lose.

POWER What about you? You were on the way to becoming a normal person. Fresh air. Sunny days. Maybe even something daring like a love affair with someone you weren't related to. Sad.

MARGARET [*sobbing*]. It's not sad. I love him! I can't help loving him. I don't like loving him. I hate loving him. Help me. Won't someone help me. [BRIGOT *goes to her, hugs her.*]

BRIGOT I'm sorry I sent her, Power. I didn't mean to hurt her. It was my way of fighting back. I knew you'd think that if Margaret was trying to lead you away from anything it would be from her brother. And her brother was tied-in with Sam and Sam was trying to set me up.

POWER But in the meantime Sam was being set up.

SAM By whom?

POWER Yourself. Because you also sent Susan Long to see me. But you didn't know it was Margaret. Goodbye, Sam. It's been great.

SAM Where am I going?

POWER Outside to give yourself up to the police.

SAM You have nothing connecting me to any crime.

POWER Anna, who helped you to dispose of Norman's body?

ANNA I'm not saying.

POWER All right a deal. I'll forget to mention that it was you who poisoned Peter's food.

BAXTER You mean he's dead?

POWER Oh yes. A slow-working poison. Fainted first. Died about two minutes ago. That reminds me. I need eighty bucks.

BAXTER What for?

POWER To pay the chef. He's a private detective. He saw her do it. Passed me along a note in my champagne creole. The poison of course was meant for me.

BAXTER Pretty cold-hearted of you to just let him die.

POWER True. But I needed the leverage. [*To* ANNA.] Two murders. Or one murder, Anna. You don't owe him anything.

ANNA Sam helped me to get rid of Norman's body. We took their father's boat out late at night.

SAM [*standing*]. Leave my father out of this!

POWER [*and* SAM *and* BAXTER] He was a great man!

POWER Goodbye, Sam. [SAM *goes to* POWER, *drink in hand. Turns and throws it in* BAXTER's *face.*]

SAM [*To* MARGARET.] Goddamnit! I knew I knew you from somewhere! [*Leaves.*]

POWER Goodbye, Anna. I hope your stay in prison isn't too tough on you.

ANNA I'll survive. [*Leaves.*]

BAXTER You're getting awfully good at this, Tyrone.

POWER Yeah. Allan, be a good little witness and get your ass out there, will you. [ALLAN *nods. Stands.*]

ALLAN Remember your promise or I won't testify.

POWER Don't worry. [ALLAN *runs off.*]

BAXTER You bought him with a promise?

POWER Yeah. That I'd help him get his Actor's Equity card.

BRIGOT An Equity card. Loyalty is cheap. Everywhere except Amframica.

POWER And in the capital. Where it is very expensive. Where some people play with their sanity. Right, Margaret? [MARGARET *ignores him.* POWER *sits down. Leans back in his chair.*] Double scotch, Baxter. [BAXTER *goes to the liquor table.*] Brigot, I forgot to thank you for that telephone call and the information the other night.

BRIGOT Have you done anything about it yet?

POWER No. But the night is young.

BRIGOT Not for me. [*Stands.*] Is there a back way out of here? I hate crowds.

POWER   [*points*]. Goodbye Brigot. You're a strange lady. But I like you.

BRIGOT   Well I don't like you, Power. You're a cynic. And you went out of your way to make me look like a fool when you knew deep inside that I was harmless. [*She leaves.* MARGARET *has put on sunglasses. And is preparing to leave.*]

POWER   Good enough, Margaret. The press won't recognize you if that's all you're worrying about.

MARGARET   It wouldn't be good for Paul or me to be involved in any of this.

POWER   I told you. He's finished. I've got him.

MARGARET   You won't hurt him. You love me. And you know I love him. [*Laughs.*]

POWER   Margaret. Look at me. You're not well.

MARGARET   It's just that I'm in love with my brother. And it's making me a bit tense.

POWER   You should do something about it. It's making you do some very peculiar things.

MARGARET   Help me.

POWER   I can't. I tried.

MARGARET   You did? You should have tried harder. [*She starts off.*] You should have tried much harder. [*Leaves.*]

BAXTER   Do you think she'll be back?

POWER   Not for a while. Her psychiatrist is waiting outside. He's going to have her committed.

BAXTER   That's sad.

POWER   I know. [BAXTER *brings* POWER *his martini.* POWER *drinks it.*] Well I guess I might as well go home. Goodnight. [*Starts off.*]

BAXTER   Wait, Power. You've forgotten something, haven't you?

POWER   What?

BAXTER   Who killed Bitch Nelson?

POWER   Oh yeah.

BAXTER   Do you know?

POWER   No. Haven't got a clue. Sorry. Does that mean I won't get my column back?

BAXTER   Well, you've solved just about everything else. Got a lot of celebrities in the news. It'll sell a lot of newspapers. Yeah. You can have your column back.

POWER   Feel bad about the Bitch Nelson thing though. Just

couldn't get a handle on it – [*He starts off.*]

BAXTER Probably a crime of passion ... or something.

POWER [*Stops in his tracks. Pause. He turns and looks at* BAXTER. *Moves slowly towards him.*] Just how drunk are you, Baxter?

BAXTER Oh don't worry. I can make it home all right.

POWER That's not why I ask. You've been drinking from this bottle of domestic vodka all night and I just want to know how drunk you can be from drinking water. [*He takes a drink from the bottle.*] It is water you lousy son of a bitch!!

BAXTER [*Sobers up. Jumps to his feet.*] Relax, Power.

POWER Shut up. What the hell were you trying to pull anyway?

BAXTER I thought if I pretended to be drunk I'd learn more.

POWER Wrong. Try again.

BAXTER Look Power, just remember who's boss here.

POWER That's no good either. Why was I put on the Bitch Nelson murder?

BAXTER I told you it would sell newspapers.

POWER That call I got offering information the other night was from Brigot Nelson. Your father didn't really die as legend has it, of terminal greed, he actually committed suicide.

BAXTER That's not true.

POWER He was driven to suicide.

BAXTER That's vicious gossip.

POWER He had political ambitions and someone prevented him from realizing them. That someone was Margaret's brother Paul. Paul destroyed your father.

BAXTER Lies.

POWER The truth. And all I had to do was figure out what it meant.

BAXTER It's a story. It doesn't mean anything.

POWER A story about revenge. It means that you wanted it so badly that I was put on the Bitch Nelson murder because you knew that if I started investigating her crowd that eventually I would be led to Margaret's brother. And that I would do everything I could to destroy him because of how I felt about Margaret.

BAXTER You're fantasizing, Power.

POWER It also means that you were so demented and hungry for revenge that you'd do anything to get me involved with Bitch Nelson's crowd in the first place.

BAXTER I'm warning you, Power.

POWER I'm immune, Baxter. I've been warned right into indifference. Now admit it. Admit that you killed Jane Nelson.

BAXTER Are you crazy? You can't blame it on me just because I'm the only one left. [*He laughs.*]

POWER Shut up. I've been had. You used me, Baxter. You used me more than anyone has ever used me in my whole life. You were the one disguised as Pedro Puchinsky that night at the art gallery.

BAXTER [*laughing*]. I was not.

POWER I've had enough Baxter. Now admit it, you demented bastard, or I'll tell the whole world about your great courageous father! [*The gun that* ALLAN *gave* POWER *is still on the table.* BAXTER *lunges for it.* POWER *grabs him. Somehow they wind up on top of the table struggling with the gun. It goes off. They separate. Look at each other with concern.*]

BAXTER Okay, I did it! So what?!

POWER Whatya mean, so what?

BAXTER Don't get excited, Power. It's not like I do it for a hobby. It was necessary this one time. That's all.

POWER What a marvellous attitude. What a better place the world would be if all cold-blooded killers were like you, Baxter.

BAXTER I underestimated you. I thought you'd be satisfied getting Margaret's brother.

POWER I was. This was just an afterthought.

BAXTER What do you mean? When exactly did you find out?

POWER Just now. I was guessing. [*Laughs.*]

BAXTER [*laughs*]. Then nobody else knows.

POWER I was guessing.

BAXTER And you can't prove it, can you.

POWER I was guessing. But I had suspicions. And I took precautions.

BAXTER Like what?

BELLUM [*Lifts his head out of the chicken champagne creole.*] A witness!

POWER Did you hear?

BELLUM Everything.

POWER Good. The police are outside. Just repeat it all to them and

71

they'll go easy on you just like I promised.

BELLUM [*Starts off. Stops.*] Oh by the way. Honestly and when I say honestly I mean reasonably honestly, what did you think of my performance as a whole and more specifically, if you don't mind, my death scene.

POWER I thought it was ... more or less ... just about ... the way it was.

BELLUM Precisely. [*He leaves.* BAXTER *shakes* POWER's *hand. Turns to go.* POWER *stops him.*]

POWER Where are you going, Baxter?

BAXTER Outside. To give myself up. [POWER *sits down at the head of the table.*]

POWER Later, Baxter, later. Something terrible happened to me today. My dog died. He just relieved himself one final time in the hallway then fell down and died. And now that Margaret's gone you're just about the only friend, so to speak, I have. Let's have a drink or two to the good old times we had together.

BAXTER We didn't have any.

POWER Let's pretend.

BAXTER For how long, Power? [*Long pause.*]

POWER For as long as it takes me to forget about my dog. [*They look at each other.* BAXTER *shrugs. Leaves.* POWER *raises a glass to the empty table. Slouches down in his chair.*]
BLACKOUT
END

Filthy Rich

Filthy Rich was first produced by Toronto Free Theatre, Toronto, in January 1979, with the following cast:

TYRONE M. POWER. David Bolt
JAMIE MCLEAN. Angelo Rizacos
ANNE SCOTT. Nancy Beatty
SUSAN SCOTT. Janet-Laine Green
POLICE DETECTIVE STACKHOUSE. Richard Donat
HENRY 'THE PIG' DUVALL. Steven Bush

Directed by William Lane
Designed by Brian Arnott and Syvalya Elchen
Original Score composed by John Roby

Persons in the Play
TYRONE M. POWER
JAMIE MCLEAN
ANNE SCOTT
SUSAN SCOTT
POLICE DETECTIVE STACKHOUSE
HENRY 'THE PIG' DUVALL

Scene One

Late evening. POWER's *office in a dirty old building in a dirty old part of the city. The office is a mess. Books and things, crumpled-up papers all over the place. A desk, a couple of chairs, a cot. And an aquarium with four or five fish.*

    POWER *is sitting at his desk. Staring at his typewriter. The man is middle-aged and balding. Walrus mustache. Thick-rimmed glasses. A bit overweight. Occasionally he types a few words. Mostly he stares. Muffled sounds of a city at night outside. An ambulance goes by.* POWER *stands, looks out the window. Stretches. Turns. Picks his pipe up from the desk. Lights it. Goes over to his aquarium. Feeds the fish. There is a half-empty bottle of whiskey on his desk.* POWER *is quite drunk. A knock at the door.* POWER *looks. Says nothing. Feeds his fish some more. Another and the door opens and* JAMIE *in a partial messenger's uniform comes it.*

JAMIE Your name Power?

POWER Yes.

JAMIE How come you don't answer your door?

POWER I was thinking about it. How come you open doors before they're answered.

JAMIE Because I'm a busy man. The office has been trying to reach you for hours. You don't answer your phone either. But I guess you think about it though, eh.

POWER Sometimes.

JAMIE A man of action. You should get into politics. The world needs people like you.

POWER Correct me if I'm wrong, I've been drinking just a little you see, but aren't you a delivery boy.

JAMIE Yeah.

POWER You have a really unusual attitude for a delivery boy.

JAMIE Oh right. I guess you'd have liked it better if I'd crawled in on my stomach.

POWER That's one approach. The other is to just deliver what it is you're supposed to deliver without all the commentary.

JAMIE It's a telegram. Are you really a private eye.

POWER No.

JAMIE It's addressed to Tyrone M. Power. Private Eye.

POWER It's from my mother. She's [*he takes a drink*] a romantic.

JAMIE Your name really Tyrone Power? You gotta be kidding.

POWER I told you. My mother's a romantic. Read it.

JAMIE That's not my job.

POWER Read it. To yourself. Then read it to me. Unless it's bad news. If it's bad news I want you to just take it away with you when you leave. I've had enough of the stuff.

JAMIE I told you that's not my job.

POWER Look. Do what I tell you or I'll throw you out the goddamn window.

JAMIE Listen, you stupid drunk. Who the hell do you think you're talking to. I only do this part time you know. I'm not one of those lackey-jerks you can step on because you're in a bad mood. I do work like this to put myself through school. In short I'm an intelligent and educated human being.

POWER Well that's different, isn't it. Now please do as I've asked you or I'll shove the entire collected works of Thomas Mann down your throat.

JAMIE [*Opens telegram. Reads it.*] Your cousin Peter is dead. [POWER*'s head slumps. He puts his hands in his pockets. Walks to window.*]

POWER [*sadly*]. He was my age. That's the third relative this year. Plus two reasonably close friends. They're dropping like flies. Must be some kind of mysterious plague or something. [*Pause, he turns to* JAMIE.] I guess you didn't understand. I asked you not to tell me if it was bad news. [*Slumps in his chair, takes a drink, starts to cry.*]

JAMIE I thought you needed to be taught a lesson. How was I to know you were going to take it so badly. I'm sorry. [*Leaves.*]

POWER No. You're not. You didn't even know him. I didn't really know him either. But that's not the point, is it. [*Stares at the paper in the typewriter. Leans forward. Reads.*] I've said that already. I said that in Chapter One. What's wrong with my mind. It's drunk. Shut up, Power. Well it is drunk. Shut up, Power. [*Rips the paper from the typewriter.*

Crumples it. Throws it away. Takes another long drink. Begins to put another piece of paper in the typewriter. Changes his mind. Throws it away.] No. It's time for change. An innovation. A new literary form. The invisible novel. [*Begins to type furiously on the paperless typewriter.*] Something indicative of the age in which we live. Sold in drugstores. Buried in time capsules. Read in subways. The invisible novel. No effort here. Mass marketing. Buy yours now. Or don't. Who'll know. Shut up Power. You're self-destructing. Ignore him Power. Self-destruction is good for you. It makes your usual state of obscene neutrality seem almost euphoric. Oh please do shut up Power. Chapter Two. The invisible hero. Chat Northcott, a professional architect, blood pounding in his veins over the loss of the lady with quaint charms whose name was ... whose name was ... was any one of those silly names from one of those silly books ... [*The door opens. A lady. Very attractive. Very expensively dressed, comes in.*]

ANNE   Hello. My name is Anne Scott.

POWER   Yes. That'll do. [*He types.*] Whose silly name is Anne Scott.

ANNE   I beg your pardon. [POWER *puts his head on his typewriter. Leaves it there. She watches him for a while.*] Are you all right. [POWER *lifts his head slowly.*]

POWER   Death in the family.

ANNE   I'm sorry.

POWER   Yes you should be. It was *your* family. [*He laughs, pounds the typewriter.*] Got you didn't I. Teach you not to use artificial expressions of sympathy as a conversational tool. Make you a more acceptable person in circles where that kind of thing is noticed. Mental health clinics, line ups for European films –

ANNE   Please shut up.

POWER   What?

ANNE   I have no idea what you're talking about.

POWER   Oh. Small joke. Bad taste. Difficult time. No money. Everyone dying. Strange mood. And quite drunk too.

ANNE   Yes. I've noticed. Do you think you could possibly manage to sober up for just a moment. I have something important to ask you.

POWER   Sorry. I can't deal with anything important.

ANNE   Perhaps you could if you were sober.

POWER   That happens to be the reason I'm not sober.

ANNE   Please, Mr. Power.

POWER   Okay. Give me a minute. I've got a trick. [*He goes to window. Stares out. Rubs his head.*]

ANNE   I'm here because of an old friend of yours.

POWER   Shush. One minute. I've got a trick. [*Long pause.* POWER *turns.*] I'm sober now.

ANNE   Good. I need your help badly. I'm afraid you're the only one I could turn to.

POWER   Yes I'm sober now.

ANNE   Good. I know you're not really a detective but you've had some experience in that line of work and we, that is I, well I think it's a matter of – [POWER *passes out.*] Life and death. BLACKOUT

Scene Two

Later. Down in the street, someone is playing a saxophone. Badly. POWER *is sitting on the edge of his cot. Shaking his head. Rubbing his jaw.* SUSAN SCOTT *is sitting next to him. Holding a plastic cup. She is younger than her sister. Just as expensively dressed, but more casual.*

SUSAN   Coffee.

POWER   Thanks.

SUSAN   How are you feeling.

POWER   Terrible.

SUSAN   You shouldn't drink so much. I had to slap your face for five minutes to wake you up.

POWER   Nice of you to go to so much trouble. I think you broke my jaw.

SUSAN   I thought for a while you were dead.

POWER   Who are you.

SUSAN   Susan Scott.

POWER   Any relation to Anne Scott?

SUSAN   She's my sister. Was she here.

POWER Yes.

SUSAN What did she want.

POWER What do you want.

SUSAN Please. I have to know what she told you.

POWER I don't remember. I was in the process of passing out.

SUSAN Don't get involved with her, Mr. Power. She's dangerous.

POWER I have no intention of getting involved with her.

SUSAN Good.

POWER [Gets up slowly. Goes to window. Breathes.] I have no
intention of getting involved with you either, by the way. I
say that just in case you get around to answering that
question I asked you a little while ago. You know. The one
that went, what do you want.

SUSAN I was sent here by a close friend of yours. I want you to
find a missing person.

POWER I don't have any close friends. I used to have a couple of
reasonably close friends. They died. And I don't look for
missing people. That's detective work.

SUSAN This is really important, Mr. Power. The missing person is
someone very special to me.

POWER Look. I'm not a detective. I used to be in the newspaper
business. I used to be an investigative reporter. I used to
do the kind of thing you're asking me to do for reasons I
could never figure out except that maybe my mother was
a romantic who loved pulp fiction, but what the hell did
that have to do with me, right? Anyway, I don't do those
things any more. I stay here and write my book. The same
book I've been writing for fifteen years and I make what
little money I have by writing silly freelance articles on
leisure for a silly weekend magazine. Now if you want to
know thirty-five ways people with incomes of
approximately fifteen thousand dollars spend weekends
in the months of January through October you've come to
the right place. Otherwise go get professional help.

SUSAN Believe me, I wouldn't be here if there was someone else I
could go to. Please listen to me. Someone could be killed.
A lot of people hurt.

POWER Go to the police.

SUSAN I can't. I have to be discreet.

POWER Go to a private investigator.

SUSAN   I need someone I can trust.

POWER   Buy a dog.

SUSAN   Ah, there's no reason to be glib, Mr. Power. Why won't you just listen to what I have to tell you.

POWER   It's because of the way you look.

SUSAN   Is there something wrong with my appearance?

POWER   No. But if I let them, women like you can convince me to do some pretty outrageous things. Someone who looked half as good as you for example could probably convince me to invade Central America single-handedly. And I'm just not in the mood.

SUSAN   That's a very nice compliment but –

POWER   Yeah. Well it's not so much a compliment for you as it is a statement about my stupidity. Now please go away.

SUSAN   [*Starts off. Stops.*] The missing person is Michael Harrison.

POWER   The same Michael Harrison who is running for mayor?

SUSAN   Yes.

POWER   I don't want to hear any more.

SUSAN   There are some people who want to kill him.

POWER   Of course.

SUSAN   He knows that. He's scared.

POWER   Go away.

SUSAN   He's in hiding. I have to find him. You have to help me find him.

POWER   Please. Go away.

SUSAN   But he's a very important man. He'll be a good mayor.

POWER   Yeah. Well he may still win. Don't tell anyone he's missing. He won't be the first invisible candidate to win an election. This city's got a tradition of mayors who are difficult to locate.

SUSAN   That's why we need a man like Michael Harrison.

POWER   Look. My civic conscience went down the toilet a long time ago. It wasn't an accident. I flushed it down myself when I realized it was a useless thing to have. So if you're going to keep trying, try another approach.

SUSAN   My family is very wealthy. I'll pay you well.

POWER   Go to the police. They do it for free.

SUSAN   I can't. It's a family matter. Very delicate.

POWER   [*He has opened the door for her.*] Yes. All family matters of the very rich are. Michael Harrison comes from a rich family too, doesn't he.

SUSAN Yes. Why.

POWER Just wanted to make sure I wasn't turning my back on an under-dog.

SUSAN That's not fair. Money or no money. He's a human being in trouble. You're a really mixed-up person, Mr. Power. You won't talk to me because you find me attractive and you won't help a desperate man because he happens to come from a wealthy family. You need professional counselling.

POWER Sure.

SUSAN No. I mean it. No wonder you drink yourself into unconsciousness and live in this hole. You have serious psychological problems. I feel sorry for you.

POWER Well let's not get embarrassing about it. I mean it wasn't me who brought you here lady. You came on your own initiative.

SUSAN And it was obviously a mistake. I see that now. You're totally inadequate for my needs.

POWER Terrific. Get indignant. It suits you. Goes with the expensive clothes.

SUSAN Oh shut up!

POWER Get the hell out of my office.

SUSAN Your office is a disgusting mess. Just like you. And it is a pleasure to leave you both.

POWER Well, bye bye.

SUSAN [*Takes a step. Stops.*] Oh, one more thing.

POWER What. [*She slaps him.*] What was that for?

SUSAN For wasting my time. [*She leaves.* POWER *slams the door. Sits down. Stands. Goes to the window. Leans out.*]

POWER Excuse me! I've been meaning to tell you for the past five months how really badly you play that instrument! You have no talent! You're a fake! Fake! [*Saxophone sputters. Stops.* POWER *slams the window. Looks around. Sits down at his desk. Stares at the typewriter.*] Fake.

BLACKOUT

Scene Three

Later. Early evening. JAMIE, *in overalls, is cleaning the office.*
Sweeping, emptying the ashtrays, etc. There are three
green garbage bags in the corner. The crumpled-up papers
are gone. POWER *comes in carrying something in a brown*
paper bag.

POWER   Who the hell are you?

JAMIE   Janitor.

POWER   Since when.

JAMIE   This is my first day.

POWER   This building hasn't had a janitor in three years.

JAMIE   [*looking around*]. Probably the happiest three years of
your life. I convinced the owner he needed me.

POWER   How?

JAMIE   I called him up and said you need me. How come your
office looks like you live in it.

POWER   Because I do.

JAMIE   [*Continues to clean.* POWER *is looking at him oddly. He sits.*
Takes a coffee and a sandwich from the bag. Crumples the
bag. Throws it on the floor. JAMIE *looks at him.*] Did you
throw that on the floor just so that I could pick it up.

POWER   No. I did it to illustrate my lifestyle.

JAMIE   What's that supposed to mean.

POWER   I like this place the way it is. I don't want it cleaned up.

JAMIE   Suit yourself. I'll just take out the garbage.

POWER   It's the garbage that I'm particularly fond of.

JAMIE   What do you do. Eat it?

POWER   No, I read it. It's my novel.

JAMIE   If it's your novel why do you treat it like garbage.

POWER   Because I belong to a literary school that believes strongly
in self-disgust. Any more questions?

JAMIE   Well excuse me for living. What am I doing, keeping you
from something important.

POWER   You look familiar. Haven't you come into my life with the sole purpose of irritating the shit out of me on some other occasion.

JAMIE I saw you last night. I brought you a telegram. It was bad news. You cried. It was pitiful.

POWER Oh right. The delivery boy. The one who's working his way through school. [*Pause.*] I cried because I was drunk, I don't usually drink so much. It was just one of those nights. I don't know why I'm telling you that. I don't know why the hell I'm even talking to you.

JAMIE Drunks talk to anyone.

POWER What's your name.

JAMIE Jamie McLean.

POWER Well Jamie. Can I call you Jamie?

JAMIE Who cares.

POWER Right. Well Jamie. You're definitely an unusual young man. I mean you have a truly unorthodox attitude towards casual conversation which would probably make you an ideal choice for a character study in some poorly made sex film. But in the real world, such as it is, you're a bit over the edge if you know what I mean. And it's no wonder at all that you got fired from your delivery job. In fact the only wonder is that you didn't have your obnoxious little brain bashed in before that happened.

JAMIE Who said anything about getting fired, you pompous long-winded asshole. That was my night job. This is my day job.

POWER Yeah. Well just stay out of my way or it might be your last job.

JAMIE Tough talk from a drunk who calls himself Tyrone Power, tells his mother he's a private eye and writes novels he keeps in green garbage bags. Real tough talk. [*Leaves. Slams door.*]

POWER You're damn right. [*Pause.*] Oh Jesus. I forgot to feed the fish. [*He starts towards the aquarium. Phone rings. Twice.* POWER *picks up receiver.*] Hello. [*Pause.*] Hello. [*Pause. He hangs up. Looks worried. Goes to aquarium.* DETECTIVE STACKHOUSE *comes in.*]

STACKHOUSE You Power?

POWER Yes.

STACKHOUSE My name is Stackhouse.

POWER   Hello.

STACKHOUSE   I'd like to ask you a few questions.

POWER   Would you mind telling me who you are first.

STACKHOUSE   I'm the law, Power.

POWER   Oh. You mean you're a policeman.

STACKHOUSE   That's what I said.

POWER   No. You said 'I'm the law.' Which is sort of like saying I'm the truth. Or I'm wisdom. Or I'm the god of the Bountiful Harvest.

STACKHOUSE   What in God's name are you going on about.

POWER   Well it seems to me that there has been a trend developing recently where people come through that door and say some of the stupidest things I've ever heard in my life and I just thought it was time I started to point them out.

STACKHOUSE   All right. You've made your point. Now sit down. [POWER *sits.*] Where's Michael Harrison?

POWER   [*groans*]. Do you know what life is? Life is a series of apparent coincidences contrived by mysterious forces to make sane men like me crazy.

STACKHOUSE   Where is Michael Harrison, Power.

POWER   I suppose you're going to keep asking me that question until I give you an answer.

STACKHOUSE   That's right.

POWER   Okay. Michael Harrison is in Calcutta. He's had an immense and painful pang of conscience. He's in Calcutta giving all of his considerable wealth to the dismal poor, in whom he has until now shown absolutely no interest. Which will probably make it impossible for you to believe this story unless you go right now to Calcutta without stopping to say another fatuous word to me.

STACKHOUSE   You talk a lot.

POWER   I talk a lot when I'm nervous. Or agitated. I get nervous and agitated when I'm asked questions about things I know nothing about.

STACKHOUSE   I was told you know where he is.

POWER   By whom?

STACKHOUSE   Reliable sources.

POWER   Name them.

STACKHOUSE   No. You've got it all wrong. You don't tell me. I tell you.

POWER   Not unless you've got a charge.

Scene Three

STACKHOUSE Look Power. This is a big city. We have what you might call a high national profile. Now we're having an election for mayor. And one of the candidates is missing. It's not public knowledge yet but it's a pretty hard thing to hide. And when it gets out it's going to be a touch embarrassing for a lot of people. My bosses included. So I have a great amount of pressure on me and I am very willing to apply an even greater amount of pressure on you unless you tell me straight and clean what you know.

POWER Was it either one of the Scott sisters who sent you here.

STACKHOUSE What have they got to do with it.

POWER They've both been here asking me to find Harrison. I don't know. Maybe they think I already know where he is.

STACKHOUSE With good reason if they get their information from the same people I do. He was last seen with a Fred Whittacker. Mr. Whittacker is a friend of yours isn't he.

POWER He used to be.

STACKHOUSE Whatya mean?

POWER We were in the newspaper business together. In fact we were sort of partners at one time. The political beat.

STACKHOUSE Do you know where he is now.

POWER He used to live in that hotel across from city hall.

STACKHOUSE I'm talking about where he is now. This minute. He hasn't been seen at the hotel since Harrison disappeared.

POWER Well I haven't seen him in years. We had a falling out.

STACKHOUSE About what?

POWER None of your business.

STACKHOUSE Look Power. Take the direct route. Save your fancy moves for your love life, if you have one, and answer the questions as they're asked.

POWER We were close. We worked on the job. The job involved a lot of devious important stuff. I left because I thought it was futile nonsense. He stayed because he thought it wasn't. Two different choices. Seemed to imply certain things about our personalities that put a strain on the relationship. I guess you can understand that can't you.

STACKHOUSE Oh, yeah, I can understand it. I just don't know if I can believe it.

POWER Well that's your problem. Go away and mull it over. Take all the time you want. Take years.

STACKHOUSE	Your name and phone number were found in his hotel room.
POWER	So what? In some little address book along with a couple of dozen others probably.
STACKHOUSE	All by itself. Written on Friday's newspaper.
POWER	How convenient.
STACKHOUSE	Not for you. What is the Scott family interest in Harrison.
POWER	I don't know that it is a family interest. It might be more personal.
STACKHOUSE	Either of them involved with him romantically?
POWER	Maybe.
STACKHOUSE	What do you mean maybe, Power. Let's hear it straight.
POWER	Maybe's the best I can do. On all counts. I don't know anything about any of this.
STACKHOUSE	Or maybe you just don't know how serious this business is. Or maybe you're just being cute.
POWER	Really. Do you think I'm cute?
STACKHOUSE	Very cute.
POWER	Thanks. You know I think you're kinda cute yourself. But we better be careful how far we take this because this is only our first date.
STACKHOUSE	That's right. And I don't like getting screwed on a first date. Besides, I meant cute as in dishonest. No offense. I know it's just a tradition for people in your business. I understand.
POWER	My business is writing. I write.
STACKHOUSE	You have something of a reputation as a snoop.
POWER	The old days. All gone. I write. I live here well below the starvation level in this dirty old building in this dirty old part of the city with dirty and poor people down in the street and I write. I write and I mind my own business. I don't get involved with the dirty poor and they're at least worth getting involved with, and if I don't get involved with the dirty poor I sure as hell don't get involved with the filthy rich. I'm a cynic. Get it? A cynic doesn't get involved with anything. It took me years to get this way and I have no intention of changing for anyone. I'm not happy. But I'm immune.
STACKHOUSE	You talk a lot.
POWER	Only when people seem to have trouble understanding what I'm saying. It's a belief in quantity over clarity.

Scene Three

STACKHOUSE You talk a lot. And you don't say anything. Maybe it's the atmosphere. Maybe you need a change. Let's go.

POWER Where?

STACKHOUSE My office.

POWER Are you arresting me?

STACKHOUSE You got it.

POWER Why.

STACKHOUSE You're my only lead. You may not be much. But I'm going to milk you dry until I get another one.

POWER And what's the charge.

STACKHOUSE What's it matter?

POWER Hey, Stackhouse. The golden age of seize and destroy is over. I've got rights.

STACKHOUSE Oh yeah. I forgot ... Practising without a licence.

POWER Practising what.

STACKHOUSE Private investigation.

POWER That's not a criminal offense. It's a licensing infraction. Send me a summons.

STACKHOUSE Wait. I think I've got something better. [*Goes calmly to the door. Opens it. Turns. Looks around. Picks up a chair. Breaks it over* POWER's *desk. Yells. Rips open his own coat. Tears his own shirt. Takes his hat off. Throws it on the floor. Steps on it. Looks at* POWER. *Smiles. They stare at each other for a moment.*] Assaulting a police officer.

POWER Oh for chrissake. You know what life is?

STACKHOUSE [*has the door open*]. Get your coat.

POWER [*gets his coat*]. Life is a conspiracy by people like you to turn the simple into the complex, the obvious into the mysterious and the mentally healthy into those funny old people who scratch around in public trash cans.

STACKHOUSE [*They are walking through the door.*] Aren't you going to turn off the lights.

POWER No.

STACKHOUSE I think you should, you know. We're in the middle of an energy crisis.

POWER Screw the energy crisis. [*Leaves.* STACKHOUSE *shrugs. He flicks the switch.*]
BLACKOUT

Scene Four

Early evening. JAMIE, *in his delivery boy uniform, is sitting with his feet up, at* POWER'*s desk. Eating an apple. Reading* POWER'*s garbage. Snickering.* ANNE SCOTT, *in expensive evening clothes, is pacing.*

ANNE I can't wait much longer.

JAMIE Relax. He's probably just gone out for coffee. His kind never goes far from home. He's part of the bomb-shelter generation.

ANNE Who did you say you were.

JAMIE You didn't ask.

ANNE I really can't wait much longer. Someone is waiting downstairs for me.

JAMIE Then leave.

ANNE I have to talk to Mr. Power.

JAMIE About a case?

ANNE A what?

JAMIE A case. Are you hiring him to do something for you?

ANNE I don't know. I was going to. But last night when I came to discuss the matter with him he behaved – I mean he was – tell me, does Mr. Power have a chronic drinking problem.

JAMIE He's a drunk.

ANNE Yes. That's what I thought.

JAMIE A disgusting drunk.

ANNE Yes. Not a very reliable type.

JAMIE Relax. All good private detectives are disgusting drunks. It has something to do with self-hatred conflicting with high moral standards of a rigid upbringing or something. They all suffer from it.

ANNE Perhaps they're all Presbyterians.

JAMIE I see you've got a sense of humour. I like that. I see you're a very classy lady. I like that too.

ANNE You do.

JAMIE You bet.

ANNE That's nice. But who are you.

JAMIE I'll ask the questions for now.

ANNE But I see no reason to answer them if you don't tell me who you are.

JAMIE I might be the man you've been looking for to solve all your problems.

ANNE What a terrifying thought.

JAMIE Hey, I said I liked you but that doesn't mean you can insult me. You rich people are all alike.

ANNE We are not.

JAMIE [*stands*]. So you are rich.

ANNE Yes.

JAMIE Good. Now this case you were going to put Power on. Were you going to pay him a lot.

ANNE Yes.

JAMIE How much.

ANNE Well frankly, just about as much as he wanted.

JAMIE That could be one hell of a lot of money.

ANNE It's very important.

JAMIE And you have one hell of a lot of money?

ANNE Of course.

JAMIE On you?

ANNE No not on me. It follows me at a discreet distance.

JAMIE Right. Then you'll have to give me a cheque.

ANNE For what?

JAMIE A retainer. This is your lucky day. I'm taking your case.

ANNE That's wonderful. But who are you.

JAMIE Name is Jamie McLean. I'm an associate of Mr. Power's.

ANNE Why didn't you say so earlier.

JAMIE That's not the way it's done. There's a feeling out period first. I had to make sure of two things. One that you were serious. Because we get a lot of cranks in here. And two, that you really had the money to pay us. Because Power and McLean don't work cheap.

ANNE If you're an associate of Mr. Power's why are you wearing what appears to be a delivery boy's uniform.

JAMIE I just came off a case. Undercover. Industrial espionage.

ANNE You seem very young to be a private detective.

JAMIE And you seem very young to have a hell of a lot of money. Now do you want to talk business or not.

ANNE All right. I have to find Michael Harrison. And I have to find him before my sister does. Or anyone else. It's very

Angelo Rizacos (JAMIE), Steven Bush (HENRY)
and Nancy Beatty (ANNE)

important that when he is found that I talk to him before
he comes out of hiding.

JAMIE Okay. First things first. Who is Michael Harrison.

ANNE Don't you read the newspapers. He's running for mayor.

JAMIE Okay. Yeah. You're right.

ANNE What are you talking about.

JAMIE I was testing you. Relax. You passed.

ANNE Are you really a private detective.

JAMIE Look lady. What kind of relationship are we going to have
it you keep questioning my identity. Let's just get on with
it all right. Now where were we.

ANNE Michael Harrison went into hiding because he found out
something about –

DUVALL [HENRY DUVALL *opens the door. Stands at entrance. He is
very smooth looking. Tough, but well-dressed, with a few
flashes of bad taste. He speaks slowly, deliberately.*] I don't
like waiting very much.

ANNE I'll be right there, Pig.

DUVALL Who's he.

ANNE An associate of Mr. Power's.

DUVALL [*smiles*]. Stupid. The whole idea's stupid.

ANNE You said I could try it this way first. You promised.

DUVALL Stupid. He looks stupid. This place looks stupid.

ANNE Please, Pig. Just wait downstairs in the car.

DUVALL Okay. Two minutes.

ANNE But Pig –

DUVALL Shush. Two minutes. That's all. [*Smiles.*] But when I say
stupid, that's not what I mean. You know what I mean.
[*Long pause. He leaves.*]

JAMIE Okay. Question. Why do you call that man a pig.

ANNE Not a pig. Just Pig. That's Henry 'The Pig' Duvall.

JAMIE The gangster.

ANNE The businessman.

JAMIE Is he a friend of yours.

ANNE That's really none of your concern.

JAMIE They say he's a real killer. The last of the real killers. I mean
he's not one of those guys in the pool hall they just call
killer. He's one of those killers who really kill.

ANNE Look. I haven't got any more time. Here's a letter I wrote to
Mr. Power. I wrote it in the hopes that if he ever sobered
up he might read it and decide to help me. It tells

everything I know. Give it to him. And tell him if he wants to 'take the case' as you say, then I'll meet him tonight. At eleven.

JAMIE   Where.

ANNE   The bus station.

JAMIE   All right.

ANNE   I have to run. [*Opens the door.*]

JAMIE   Oh. One more thing. Tell your friend the pig I didn't much like him calling me stupid. Tell him if he ever calls me stupid again he'll regret it.

ANNE   If you like. But he doesn't much care for people saying things like that to him. He has a terrible temper.

JAMIE   Sure. What's he going to do. Come back up here and break my legs.

ANNE   Yes. Probably.

JAMIE   Okay. Then just tell him it wasn't a very nice way to talk to a stranger. [*She shakes her head. Leaves.* JAMIE *sits down. Takes another apple from his pocket. Takes a bite. Opens the letter, begins to read. Suddenly his eyes widen and he chokes on the apple. But keeps reading.* POWER *comes in. Tired.*]

POWER   What are you doing here. [JAMIE *still reading the letter, absent-mindedly takes out a telegram from his pocket, waves it around.*] Who is it this time.

JAMIE   [*still reading the letter*]. Your Aunt Sandra. Died suddenly while on a pleasure cruise in the Caribbean. Much love. And shared sympathy. Mother.

POWER   [*Bows his head. Walks slowly over to aquarium. Stares down at it. Long pause.*] Hi fish. Did you have a nice day. Do you want some food. Sure you do. [*Takes the top off the aquarium. Feeds them.*] And here's a little more to see you through the dark times ahead. [*Suddenly he sticks his head into the aquarium.* JAMIE *finishes the letter. Looks at* POWER. *Rushes over to him. Pulls his head out of the aquarium.*]

JAMIE   You're not mentally all there, you know that.

POWER   Go away. I want to be alone with my fish.

JAMIE   You can't commit suicide by sticking your head in an aquarium. That's the stupidest thing I've ever seen in my life.

POWER   Who said anything about suicide. I was just seeing what life is like in there. It's not bad. Lots of little stones. Little bubbles. A bit of seaweed. Sort of underwater pastoral.

JAMIE Power, you are a mess. Get a hold of yourself man. Were you close to this Aunt Sandra.

POWER Not really. It's not the individual deaths that bother me. It's the overall pattern. I wish I was a fish.

JAMIE Oh shut up with the fish stuff.

POWER Who are you to tell me to shut up? Every time I see you it's bad news or aggravation or some combination of both.

JAMIE But all that's going to change.

POWER Get out of my office.

JAMIE But I'm the man who is going to make you very rich.

POWER What are you talking about.

JAMIE Come on over here and sit down. [*Leads him to the couch.*] Is there anything I can get you.

POWER Upper right hand drawer of my desk. A bottle.

JAMIE Sorry. No booze.

POWER What?

JAMIE No booze. Booze is a thing of the past for you. Your long painful slide into the sewer of life is over.

POWER Just think a few hours ago you were nothing but a smart-ass punk. There is a god. And he uses assholes for angels. I'm impressed. Get out of my sight.

JAMIE Good. The old fighting spirit. You're going to need it.

POWER For what?

JAMIE Well while you were out doing who knows what except probably feeling sorry for yourself in public or writing your novel on other people's garbage, I was here protecting your business interests. You know Power, if you want to play private eye you've got to be here between the hours of nine and midnight. That's prime-time in the detective business.

POWER Get on with it.

JAMIE A very becoming lady with considerable financial resources came here to enlist your services. She was in a hurry because her boyfriend, a very brutal gentleman, who we will get to later, was in a car downstairs waiting for her. You were in real danger of losing the case until in a flash of imagination I passed myself off as your partner and secured for us both the possibility of a large fee for doing what the before-mentioned lady asked.

POWER   Which is?

JAMIE   It's all in this letter.

POWER   Give it here.

JAMIE   Why don't I just give it to you in point form?

POWER   First who was this before-mentioned lady?

JAMIE   Her name is Anne Scott.

POWER   Forget it.

JAMIE   Why?

POWER   Forget it. Burn the letter. Go away.

JAMIE   No sir. This is my chance to further my education at a leisurely pace. No more day jobs, night jobs or summer jobs. All in one shot. And it's your chance, besides making a lot of money, to make your mother very proud of you.

POWER   Look Jamie I can appreciate your need to get ahead. You're a slum kid. You wanna be middle-class.

JAMIE   Screw the sociology, Power. I wanna skip the middle-class and go directly to indescribable wealth.

POWER   Well do it on your own time. I've just spent twelve hours in a police station on account of Anne Scott and her charmed circle.

JAMIE   But don't you see what's happening. You're an easy target because you're standing still. You've got to stick your nose in and take the initiative. Right now you're a victim of your own indifference.

POWER   Good point.

JAMIE   You're damn right. I know your type. I've seen you all my life. You need someone like me to bring you back to consciousness. Because right now you're in a middle-age slump.

POWER   Well that's a little much.

JAMIE   Look, I've read this lady's letter. And it's full of powerful stuff. At first I thought who needs this. This is too big for little me. Then I remembered what my father used to say and it changed my mind.

POWER   That's touching. Words of fatherly wisdom motivating young son.

JAMIE   Wisdom my ass. My father used to say where's the fucking toilet. He was a wino. And I never want to be anything like him. That's what motivates me Power. What motivates you.

POWER   Nothing.

JAMIE   Wrong. I motivate you.

POWER   You do.

JAMIE   Yeah.

POWER   [*laughs*]. Okay. Let's hear the story.

JAMIE   Okay. Michael Harrison has disappeared. First everyone thought he'd had a nervous breakdown and just fallen away into the bushes. Then he gets in touch with his old friends the Scott sisters by letter and tells them he's in hiding. And he's in hiding because someone has threatened to have him assassinated. Fine, they think, we'll call in the police and get the dear boy some protection. But his letter goes on to state that under no circumstances should the police be notified because, get this Power, the person who is going to have him assassinated is his own father. The esteemed James Harrison is going to hire some killer to blow his son's head off. And for what reason besides upper-class lunacy? Because Michael the would-be mayor was handed some documents by a reporter named Whittacker –

POWER   Fred Whittacker?

JAMIE   Yeah. Anyway the documents had something to do with pay-offs to the city by various companies, and when Michael and Whittacker investigated they found out much to their amazement that all of these companies were owned by Michael's father. At which point Michael, insisting that he is the first of a long line of honest politicians, confronts the esteemed James Harrison and says 'Father, I cannot tell a lie, I'm gonna blow the lid on your dirty scam.' Which suggests that the son has never cared for the father anyway. Or maybe he thinks that the voters will view the destruction of his own father as a truly unique political manoeuvre and he will be swept into office on the strength of sheer audacity. Who knows? Anyway the father will have none of it and tells the would-be mayor that he has twenty-four hours to turn in the incriminating documents and the nosey reporter and withdraw from the election or he will be shot dead at sunrise.

POWER   Typical. All typical. They're nuts. The whole world's nuts.

JAMIE   Be quiet. And think, Power.

POWER   What's there to think about.

JAMIE   For one thing, why doesn't Michael want the police involved. Can't be because he's trying to save his father's neck. We already know that he was willing to send him to prison. No, it's because according to Anne Scott, a third party has entered the picture. An anonymous caller to Mr. Whittacker the reporter says he has information about scandalous behaviour by Michael Harrison at an earlier age. And what he wants in return for his silence is to have Michael withdraw from the election. Now Michael is in quite a fix and his behaviour becomes a bit erratic. He tells everyone 'no,' figuring that he can play for time. He has two separate entities, one known, one unknown, both looking for his head –

POWER   Wait. Run that one by me again.

JAMIE   Which one?

POWER   Michael Harrison is in a fix.

JAMIE   Yeah. Someone's trying to blackmail him. And his father's trying to kill him.

POWER   Right.

JAMIE   Right. But he still thinks he can win the day. He asks the Scott sisters to go to his father and say he will return the documents if his father will find out who the anonymous caller was. Not bad. Play one against the other. The father agrees. Sends out his minions and sooner than you know they discover there was no anonymous caller. It was Whittacker himself trying to blackmail Michael.

POWER   Wait a minute. Are you sure this is *Fred* Whittacker we're talking about.

JAMIE   Yeah, yeah, Fred Whittacker. Anyway, the father passes this on to the Scott sisters who are to pass it on to Michael at a secret rendezvous. Meanwhile the poor confused scared shitless Michael has been convinced by Whittacker to try another approach. He gives Whittacker a pile of money to buy the 'blackmailer' off. Whittacker takes the money along with the incriminating documents on the father for 'safe-keeping' and disappears. Michael makes the rendezvous with the Scott sisters and is told of Mr. Whittacker's double-cross just before a shot rings out of the darkness and narrowly misses our would-be mayor's head. Much confusion. Fear. Bedlam. Panic.

Sounds great. Wish I was there. Anyway. Michael Harrison disappears. And this is where we get the split between the Scott sisters. Each is probably convinced the other sold Michael out, for reasons unknown. Neither knows where he is now. And the only lead they have is a Mr. Tyrone M. Power of this address who it was said by Harrison was a friend of Fred Whittacker's with many favours owing.

POWER So the Scott sisters came to me thinking I might know where Whittacker was, not Michael Harrison.

JAMIE So that they could follow you to Whittacker. And retrieve the documents and the money from him and give Michael Harrison a fighting chance.

POWER Or one of them anyway. The other one wants his head.

JAMIE I say that's Susan.

POWER You haven't even met her.

JAMIE Process of elimination. Anne Scott is a classy lady. Direct. Self-assured. Not the criminal type. Susan Scott is an unknown quantity.

POWER Not to me. I've met her.

JAMIE And?

POWER Childish. Impulsive. Naive. But not the criminal type.

JAMIE Conclusion?

POWER They're both guilty. And we're the two biggest jerks on the planet if we go any farther with this.

JAMIE Shut up. We've got to make a decision. And since Anne Scott is the one who is going to be paying us I'm all for giving her the benefit of the doubt.

POWER Anne. Susan. What's it matter. A Scott sister's a Scott sister. And all the Scott sisters in the world are only here for one purpose. To drastically upset people like me.

JAMIE Put the self-pity away for awhile.

POWER I don't like any of it. It smells of misery and decay.

JAMIE Ah you'd say that about anything. It's part of your disease.

POWER No. Listen to me. I'm making sense. I'm thinking. For one thing, Fred Whittacker is an old friend. He's no blackmailer.

JAMIE We live in troubled times. Morality is a foggy foggy concept. Maybe he got tired.

POWER Of what.

JAMIE Of being poor. Don't you.

POWER Yes.

JAMIE   Well maybe Whittacker had the guts to do something about it.

POWER   But you're not listening. Listen. I said he was an old friend. Perhaps you've noticed I don't use that word much. Don't have many friends. In fact Whittacker might have been the only one I ever had. I knew him well, Jamie. He's a dedicated man. So much so that he could be a pain in the ass to anyone with normal human failings. He could never stoop to something like blackmail.

JAMIE   Nonsense. Everyone can stoop, Power. The human spine is especially designed for it. Comes from hundreds of years of bending over the trough.

POWER   You're pretty jaded for someone your age.

JAMIE   Well what am I supposed to do. Wait to be your age to be jaded. By then it just gets tough to do anything at all. No sense being a cynic unless you got the energy to use it against everything that made you one. Let's hop in Power. There's money to be made.

POWER   Not interested. But I would like a few answers just for my own security. And also to prove that all that garbage about Whittacker is untrue. I don't care what you say. Men like him don't get bought. They just don't. [*Pause.*] I mean not unless ... [*He is staring off.*]

JAMIE   What's wrong?

POWER   Nothing. [*Pause.*] You realize of course that if we go ahead with this we could wind up with metaphysical angst. Cases like this are always loaded with metaphysical angst. Or even worse. Existential nausea. Face to face with your own terrible limitations. Your own stupidity. Or loss of faith. A broken heart. Like an open wound. Terrible. Ugly. Yuk.

JAMIE   Shut up!

POWER   Why?

JAMIE   It's not necessary any more, Power. You don't have to do that any more. I'm here. And I am a positive force. I'm going to make you rise up from the living dead and be beautiful once more.

POWER   Sure. All right.

JAMIE   Say it like you mean it.

POWER   Sure. All right ... What was your arrangement with Anne Scott.

JAMIE A meeting at the bus station at eleven o'clock. She asked for you actually.

POWER Can't make it. You go. But don't let her see you. When she leaves, follow her.

JAMIE That's it?

POWER That's a beginning.

JAMIE What are you going to do.

POWER Make phone calls. I have to find Whittacker. We still have a few mutual acquaintances. He must have left a trail somewhere.

JAMIE What do you expect to find out from him.

POWER The other side of the story. The one I can believe. The one that makes sense. Get going. You haven't got much time.

JAMIE I'm on my way. [*Opens door.*] Power.

POWER What?

JAMIE I'm not so tough either. I've never hurt anyone in my life.

POWER Yeah. I guess I know that.

JAMIE I'd just like to get a few things no one ever thought I would. We can't hurt these people. They do it to themselves.

POWER It's not them I'm worried about. [*Pause.*] Jamie, you realize it really is dangerous. James Harrison is a powerful man. And obviously a touch ruthless. If he's willing to kill his own son imagine how much sleep he's going to lose just because he had to get rid of you and me. I mean if he gets upset at all it will be a pretty subtle emotional display.

JAMIE Yeah.

POWER That brutal boyfriend of Anne Scott's you mentioned earlier. Did you happen to catch his name?

JAMIE Henry Duvall.

POWER Change dangerous to suicidal. Duvall's a killer. A real killer. He uses guns and things like that.

JAMIE Yeah. So I've heard.

POWER And you still want to do this?

JAMIE Yeah. You have to admire my courage, don't you. [*Leaves. Pause.* POWER *goes to desk. Picks up receiver.*]

POWER Here lies this guy called Power. Got killed by his own dumbness. He didn't have to make that call. But his brain was in a state of numbness. [*Dials.*]

BLACKOUT

Scene Five

Later. The only light is from the desk lamp. POWER *is pacing. Waiting for the phone to ring. Suddenly a noise outside the window. A shadowy figure on the fire escape is knocking on the window. Two gun shots. The figure falls through the window exploding the glass and sprawling on the floor. The figure doesn't move. Neither does* POWER *for a moment. Eventually he stands. Moves cautiously. Looks down at corpse. Goes over to window. Looks out. Something catches his eye. He reaches out and retrieves a briefcase. Moves over to desk. Opens briefcase. Takes a large brown envelope. Throws it down on the desk. Lifts briefcase letting contents fall onto desk. There are many neatly bound stacks of money. He sits. Stares at it for awhile. Leans forward. Flips through a few stacks. Leans back. Pause.*

POWER Five. Hundred. Thousand. Dollars.
BLACKOUT

INTERMISSION

Scene Six

Reflection of a revolving ambulance light is seen outside the window. The legs of the corpse on a stretcher are just disappearing out the door. STACKHOUSE *closes the door after it. Turns to* POWER *who is standing stooped down at the aquarium. Tapping the glass with his finger.*

STACKHOUSE The name of the deceased? [*No response.*] Hey. What was the dead man's name, Power?
POWER Fred Whittacker.

100

STACKHOUSE   Well now. How come he had no identification on him. Nothing on him at all in fact. No money.

POWER   I have no idea.

STACKHOUSE   How come you didn't give his name to the homicide detectives.

POWER   Let them do their own work. They get paid for it. Besides, a Fred Whittacker to homicide is quite a different thing than a Fred Whittacker to you, Stackhouse. I know you're not working officially. Who is it that's put you on this thing.

STACKHOUSE   What makes you think I'm not working officially.

POWER   I called your office. They said you were off on a special assignment. What are you doing? Moonlighting?

STACKHOUSE   Shut up. And tell me what happened.

POWER   Someone shot him. He died. Actually someone shot him twice. Maybe he died twice too. But that's probably a bit too poetic for you to understand, isn't it.

STACKHOUSE   What was he doing here.

POWER   Maybe this is where he wanted to die.

STACKHOUSE   Sure. In the arms of an old friend. Whispering secrets.

POWER   No secrets. Just blood and broken glass.

STACKHOUSE   Look Power. You say you haven't seen the guy in months –

POWER   Years.

STACKHOUSE   Whatever. And then he shows up in the middle of the night on your fire escape just before someone kills him with two shots from a long-range rifle and you say you don't know what he was doing here. You better take a good look at your position. Whittacker was a blackmailer and God knows what else and if you were in with him –

POWER   Who told you Whittacker was a blackmailer?

STACKHOUSE   Anne Scott.

POWER   She's lying.

STACKHOUSE   What makes you say that.

POWER   I'm not telling you anything until you tell me who you're working for.

STACKHOUSE   I'm a policeman. Here's the badge. I work for the police department.

POWER   Fine. Have it your way. Let's keep dancing.

STACKHOUSE   Where's Michael Harrison.

POWER   I don't know. Did you check that Calcutta lead.

STACKHOUSE   Look Power you are beginning to annoy me in a serious way. I might just take you away for a long discussion on the matter in a more secluded spot.

POWER   A threat. An overt brutal threat. You must be desperate.

STACKHOUSE   When was the last time you had contact with either of the Scott sisters.

POWER   Last night. Anne Scott early. Susan later.

STACKHOUSE   What time later.

POWER   Midnight.

STACKHOUSE   Well right away that puts you in a very serious position.

POWER   Why?

STACKHOUSE   Susan Scott is missing.

POWER   Now that's interesting.

STACKHOUSE   Sure is. Missing since ten o'clock when she left her house. Making you the last one to see her. Did you kill her, Power.

POWER   Well you have just crossed the border from the land of the ridiculous into the land of the truly bizarre, Stackhouse. What are you trying to prove by asking me things like that. That you won your job in a lottery.

STACKHOUSE   Look Power. You seem to be awfully close to the centre around which all this garbage is spinning.

POWER   You're right. And I intend to do something about that very soon.

STACKHOUSE   What's that supposed to mean.

POWER   Well I intend to start by finding out who you're working for.

STACKHOUSE   Let go of that. It's very delicate material.

POWER   Special assignment. Give me a break. You're on someone's payroll.

STACKHOUSE   [*Attacks* POWER. *Grabs him by the collar.*] Listen shithead! I've never taken a crooked penny in my life.

POWER   Let me go. [*Pause.* STACKHOUSE *lets him go.* POWER *backs away. Looking at* STACKHOUSE *curiously. Pause. Finally he smiles.*] Well I had to find out.

STACKHOUSE   Find out what?

POWER   That you're not on the take. That you're not working for the Harrisons and Scotts and their buddies. But who are you working for, Stackhouse. Tell me. Or this conversation stops now. [*Pause.*]

STACKHOUSE   The mayor.

POWER   Ah yes. The mayor. Our retiring gentle lion of a mayor has smelled the scandal cooking and put an old friend on the case to keep it all under control and save the city he has loved for so many years from becoming the laughing stock of the western hemisphere. Is that the story.

STACKHOUSE I can't say. It's a very messy business. That's all I can say.

POWER Say more, Stackhouse. An old friend of mine died here a couple of hours ago. And it wasn't a pleasant death. It was violent and murky. Everyone thinks he's a crook. And I have to hear a lot more before I cooperate with the people who seem to be accusing him. [*Long pause.* STACKHOUSE *paces. Stops.*]

STACKHOUSE It's a story about a bad smell. About a bunch of rich powerful people pushing and screwing each other and everyone else to get a whole lot more money and power that they don't really need in the first place. It's about the way the cities in this country were first formed. Through pay-offs and favours and double-plays and connections between a select handful who never let go and who can't be gotten rid of because they were in there from day one. So even when you get an honest man like my employer is, the best he can do is hold the compromise as close to the level of decency as possible. It's a matter of history. And there's no sense trying to be specific about what crimes we're talking about. Go backward. Go forward. Turn around. It's everywhere. In every department of the city's government. In every deal every contract every decision that's ever made. The same names always appear. The Harrisons. The Scotts. A few others. And now we have the Duvalls. Organized crime's gone respectable and we have dirty old money mixing with the dirty new. So the only thing a man like the mayor can do is try to make sure that when something like this Harrison nonsense goes too far it doesn't ruin the city. That's all. We can't do more. We can't understand it because we can't talk details because we can't see the whole goddamn picture. It stinks. You're a citizen, it stinks for you. I'm a working cop and it stinks for me too. [*Pause.*]

POWER Well that's the most original argument I've ever heard in favour of civil indifference. But it doesn't excuse you or the mayor, Stackhouse. There are crooks, and there are crooks who protect crooks. For whatever reason. And meanwhile people suffer. My friend Whittacker suffered.

STACKHOUSE If you've got proof about Whittacker's innocence, tell me.

POWER No proof. An instinct. Trust.

STACKHOUSE Look. I'm just doing a job. I can't figure out anything more than that. I have to find Michael Harrison before someone blows his stupid perfectly groomed head off and we have to prosecute that someone and air the whole mess. Now maybe that's protecting crooks and that's bad. But maybe we can also clear your friend's name and sort of balance the books in a way. [*Long pause.*]

POWER In a way... Sure... Okay. From now on we go on trust. The only way I can operate is if you give me some room. I've put out a few feelers and if you give me a chance I might have some answers for you.

STACKHOUSE You've got answers now, Power. I feel it.

POWER I want to make sure.

STACKHOUSE But I've got to have something to take back to my employer. He's getting very nervous.

POWER All right. Tell him there's still a chance this whole thing can be worked out in quiet. A small chance. And that includes saving Michael Harrison, the next great gentle mayor of this city.

STACKHOUSE Sounds like a lot of effort on your part. What's in it for you.

POWER I owe Whittacker something. He gave me a gift. I don't know if he meant to give it to me. But he did. Maybe it's not a gift. Maybe it's a reward. So maybe I should earn it.

STACKHOUSE And what is this reward.

POWER Oh. Five hundred thousand dollars.

STACKHOUSE Really.

POWER A joke, Stackhouse. What would the likes of me be doing with that much money.

STACKHOUSE That's exactly how much Whittacker was supposed to have taken from Michael Harrison.

POWER Really.

STACKHOUSE [*smiles*]. Crooks protecting crooks protecting crooks. We live in troubled times.

POWER Go tell the mayor one more day.

STACKHOUSE All right. I'll see what he says. [*Starts off.*]

POWER   Have you got a number in case I have to reach you in a
           hurry.

STACKHOUSE Yeah. [*Writes something on a piece of paper. Hands it to*
            POWER.] One day, Power. That's all. I'll be waiting for your
            call. [*Starts off. Stops.*] You know there's something I've
            been meaning to ask you. Do you actually live here.

POWER   Yeah.

STACKHOUSE Why.

POWER   It was a good place to be when I was writing a novel.

STACKHOUSE Novel, eh. Any good?

POWER   Not much. Anyway I've stopped. I've retired.

STACKHOUSE Retirement. I envy you. [*Leaves.* JAMIE *sticks his head
            through the venetian blinds on the window.*]

JAMIE   Check and make sure he's gone.

POWER   What are you doing out there.

JAMIE   Taking precautions. Go check. [POWER *opens the door.
           Looks down hallway. Closes door.*]

POWER   He's gone. [JAMIE *comes through the window. He is now
           wearing an old trenchcoat. And he has* SUSAN SCOTT, *also in a
           trenchcoat, by the arm.*] What are you doing with her.

JAMIE   Long story. I need a drink. [*Goes to desk. Takes out bottle.
           Takes a long drink.*] This detective stuff can be pretty
           nerve-wracking. No wonder you're an alkie.

POWER   Where did you get that coat.

JAMIE   I traded a derelict in the park for my delivery uniform.
           This seemed to be more in keeping with my new job.

POWER   It smells terrible.

JAMIE   You get used to it after awhile.

SUSAN   [*stands*]. I want to go now.

JAMIE   Too bad! Sit down! And shut up! [*She sits.* POWER *looks at*
           JAMIE.] I tried everything else with her. She only responds
           to harsh commands.

SUSAN   I thought he was going to hurt me, Mr. Power. He's got the
           eyes of a psychopath.

POWER   He's harmless. Really.

JAMIE   She isn't. She's a killer.

SUSAN   [*stands*]. I am not.

JAMIE   Shut up!

SUSAN   Shut up yourself!

David Bolt (T.M. POWER), Janet-Laine Green (SUSAN)
and Angelo Rizacos (JAMIE)

Scene Six

JAMIE I think you've blown my cover, Power. Thanks a lot.

POWER It was time for another approach. [*Turns to* SUSAN.] Please Susan sit down and we'll have a nice discussion and clarify many wonderful but murky matters.

SUSAN I don't want to discuss anything. You have no right to keep me here.

POWER Susan! Sit down. [*She does.*] [*To* JAMIE.] Speak.

JAMIE Okay. I show up at the bus station. I hide. Anne Scott shows up. She waits. Gets annoyed. Waits some more. Gets very annoyed in a strictly high class way of course, and storms out of the station pushing over a crippled old lady in the process. I follow. She walks two blocks and gets into the car of her waiting boyfriend.

POWER Henry 'The Pig' Duvall.

JAMIE A legend in his own time.

POWER The last of a disgusting breed.

JAMIE But a sweet guy once you get to know him.

POWER And it looks like Anne got to know him all right. I checked that out. [*To* SUSAN.] Oh. There's a rumour going around that Duvall has been involved with one of the Scott sisters for some time. [*To* JAMIE.] Go on.

JAMIE They drive off. I hail a cab. Follow that car, I say to the driver. He takes a whiff of my coat, gives me the once-over, and laughs for two minutes. But in the meantime, we're following. They drive around for a while then head up north to the land of the big houses and pull into a driveway at the end of which there is a mailbox with the name James Harrison on it. I leave my cab ticking away. Sneak up for a closer look. Through the living room window I see Anne Scott, James Harrison and The Pig. They're talking. No one looks happy. For some reason this makes me feel good. Anyway, I'm about to leave when I hear someone coming. I duck behind some hedges. And this young lady comes up to the window, takes out a pistol and points. I jump out of the hedges. Grab the gun, put a hand over her mouth and yank her away. I'm thinking of turning her in to the police when something crosses my mind. You know I think I have a natural talent for this business, Power.

POWER Obviously.

JAMIE I search her pockets. Find a wallet. The identification and
the name Susan Scott. So I take her back to the cab. And
here we are. Here's her gun. [*Puts it on the desk.*] And
where's the eighteen dollars.

POWER What eighteen dollars.

JAMIE To pay the cab driver. He's waiting downstairs.

POWER [*Digs in his pocket. Hands* JAMIE *some money.*] All I've got is
six-fifty. You pay the rest.

JAMIE No way. Come on.

POWER That's all I've got.

JAMIE [*sighs*]. Okay. [*Searches pockets.*] I've only got eight bucks.
That's fourteen fifty. We're three-fifty short.

POWER I've got some rolled up pennies.

SUSAN Oh for God's sake. [*Hands* POWER *a bill.*] Here. Keep the
change.

POWER [*hands it to* JAMIE]. Here. Keep the change.

JAMIE Thanks. I'll be right back. Be careful with her. I saw her
expression when she was pointing that gun. She meant it.
She looked deranged. [*Leaves.* POWER *pours himself a
drink.*]

POWER Which one of them were you going to shoot.

SUSAN What does it matter.

POWER Well I wouldn't want to think it was your sister. That
might imply a particularly nasty kind of hatred based only
on who got to sit longest on daddy's knee or something.

SUSAN I got to sit longest, Power. Daddy had good taste. Anne has
always had a strong streak of evil in her. But it wasn't her I
was going to shoot. It was Henry Duvall.

POWER Why?

SUSAN He's the one that's trying to kill Michael.

POWER Strictly on his own?

SUSAN No. But he'll be pulling the trigger. The other two will just
supply the moral support.

POWER A strange triad we have here. Your sister, a gangster and a
millionaire.

SUSAN It's all very simple, Power. If you'd let me talk to you last
night –

POWER Forget last night. I was someone else then. Go ahead.

SUSAN Duvall is Anne's boyfriend and James Harrison is Duvall's boss. If Harrison goes down so does Duvall and Anne for reasons all of her own is in love with the guy.

POWER So why does Michael Harrison mean so much to you?

SUSAN He's an old friend.

POWER Not a lover?

SUSAN We were kids together. I love him all right. But as a friend. Can you help him.

POWER Maybe.

SUSAN Do you know where he is.

POWER Maybe.

SUSAN Where.

POWER You don't have to know that. Just relax.

SUSAN I'll try. Hey, can I have a drink.

POWER Why? Do you need one.

SUSAN It's not a matter of needing one. I'd just like one.

POWER Sorry. That's my special stock. Only for people who need it. There are a few bars uptown that specialize in serving people who actually like it.

SUSAN You really are one of the most unpleasant people I have ever met.

POWER Really. Must have something to do with our personal chemistry. Just about everyone else thinks I'm wonderful. [*Pause.*] What do you know about a Fred Whittacker.

SUSAN He was a cheap con-man wasn't he.

POWER What do you mean 'wasn't he'.

SUSAN He's dead.

POWER How do you know that.

SUSAN I was on the fire escape earlier. I heard you talking to that policeman.

POWER Oh. Right. [JAMIE *comes in.*]

JAMIE Did she confess.

POWER She's innocent.

JAMIE Like hell she is!

POWER Relax.

JAMIE I don't want to relax. I want to make sure you're not jumping to conclusions. This woman carries a gun, Power.

POWER Look. It's very simple. Anne and Duvall are the bad guys. Susan was going to shoot them. Therefore, Susan is the good guy. Process of elimination. Get it?

JAMIE Yeah. And I really liked the patronizing way you put it, too.

POWER Good. Susan, can you wait outside in the hall for a minute. I want to talk to my friend.

SUSAN Oh. Okay. [*Smiles. Leaves.*]

JAMIE What is it?

POWER How long were you on the fire escape.

JAMIE Why.

POWER Did you hear that Whittacker is dead.

JAMIE No. I didn't. I'm sorry. When? How?

POWER Forget it.

JAMIE You must feel pretty bad, I mean –

POWER Never mind. Listen. It's important that we keep all of this very quiet. I want you to stay with Susan. Don't let her talk to or call anyone.

JAMIE Why?

POWER Trust me. And we both might be very rich.

JAMIE I don't see how when it turns out that our client is in with the villains.

POWER I have another source of remuneration.

JAMIE Yeah. What is it.

POWER Half a million.

JAMIE Holy shit! You're kidding. Holy shit! You're not kidding. Where is it. Let me see it. Let me touch it.

POWER Calm down.

JAMIE No way am I calming down. I'd be upsetting my natural rhythms. I feel a burst of hysteria coming on. Where did you get it.

POWER From Whittacker. He was carrying it when he was killed.

JAMIE The blackmail money from Harrison?

POWER Looks like it. Anyway, it was his and now it's mine.

JAMIE Ours.

POWER Sure. The only thing is, it came from Whittacker. It has to mean something.

JAMIE It doesn't mean anything. It's money. You buy things with it that mean something.

POWER Maybe it means I should use it against them somehow.

JAMIE Without losing it though, eh Power. Without blowing it away just to get something weird like revenge or something.

POWER Right. Don't worry. The secret, I guess, is to catch the culprits and keep the loot. [*Grabs his coat. Opens door.*]

JAMIE How do we do that.

POWER Carefully.

JAMIE Where are you going.

POWER I found a book of matches in Whittacker's pocket. It was from a hotel in the west-end. I'm going to check it out.

JAMIE Harrison?

POWER Maybe. Remember. Keep an eye on Susan. And stay put. [*Leaves.* SUSAN *comes in.* JAMIE *watches her, she watches him. An awkward moment, mostly for* JAMIE.]

SUSAN Drink?

JAMIE Sure. [*Pours her a drink. Hands it to her. She takes it down in one mouthful. Long pause.*]

SUSAN So what are we supposed to do now.

JAMIE Nothing.

SUSAN Well this is the perfect place for it. [*Smiles. He fidgets.*]

JAMIE Yeah. It's pretty pitiful isn't it. He lives here you know.

SUSAN Really? All alone?

JAMIE Yeah. Well. With his fish. And his garbage. And his broken window. And his freelance articles on things like the leisure habits of doctors' wives. I've read a couple. They stink. Hates his work obviously. Hasn't got any friends. All his relatives are dying. Generally speaking, a pretty pitiful situation. [*Pause.*] I guess he's in hiding.

SUSAN From what.

JAMIE Everything. It's typical of his age group. Fear of technology.

SUSAN No. Fear of what's-it-called. Responsibility.

JAMIE What would you know about responsibility. You have money.

SUSAN There can be a lot of responsibility in having money.

JAMIE Like what.

SUSAN How to spend it.

JAMIE Well at least you've got a sense of humour about it.

SUSAN What am I supposed to do. Offer apologies? If you had money would you apologize for it.

JAMIE No. [*Pause. She holds out her glass. He fills it. She drinks some, hands it to him. He drinks the rest.*]

SUSAN Listen. I think I should thank you for stopping me from using that gun.

111

JAMIE That's all right.

SUSAN No I'd really like to thank you. Somehow. Listen why don't you let me take you home and give you something to eat. Something a little better to drink. Some nice music. We have a very comfortable little guest house, a converted coach house I use for special occasions.

JAMIE A little charity?

SUSAN Don't be like that. I'd just like to thank you. That's all.

JAMIE Power said to sit and wait.

SUSAN Well we can sit and wait there. But we can do it so much more comfortably. What do you say.

JAMIE I don't know. [*Pause.*] Why are you looking at me like that. [SUSAN *smiles.*] Oh.

SUSAN What do you say.

JAMIE I'll leave him a note.

SUSAN [*as* JAMIE *writes*]. You'll like it there. It's very secluded. Lots of trees. A fireplace. You must be a bit unnerved by all of this. I know I am. It'll be nice to have someone to talk to. There are a lot of questions I'd like to ask you. Mr. Power is so tight-lipped.

JAMIE Yeah. Well I can't talk about the case either.

SUSAN You can trust me.

JAMIE That's not how it's done.

SUSAN Really. How *is* it done. [*Moves closer.*]

JAMIE You're very good looking. I guess you know that, eh.

SUSAN Yes. But it's nice of you to remind me.

JAMIE Let's go.

SUSAN With pleasure. [*They step out door.*] Oh I forgot my purse. [*She comes in, grabs purse and the note* JAMIE *has left for* POWER. *She puts note in purse. Starts out of door.*]
BLACKOUT

Scene Seven

ANNE SCOTT *and* POWER *coming down the hall. A muffled conversation something like this: 'Let go of my arm.' 'Shut up.' 'I said let go of my arm.' 'And I said shut up.' They come into the office.* POWER *has* ANNE *by the arm.* ANNE *is wearing a fur coat over a nightgown.* POWER *is holding a bloodied handkerchief to his nose.*

POWER Sit down over there. And be quiet. [*She looks at him. Pause. Then she sits.* POWER *looks around the office, perhaps for clues to* JAMIE *and* SUSAN*'s disappearance.*]

ANNE You realize of course that this could be interpreted as kidnapping.

POWER Nonsense. I just wanted a little friendly conversation.

ANNE Then why couldn't we have had it at my house.

POWER I don't like to be away from this place for very long. I'm worried about squatters. Besides I thought it was about time I brought you and your sister together for a little game of who's screwing who. But she seems to have vanished. I don't suppose you know where to, eh?

ANNE No I don't.

POWER Okay. Well then it's just you and me. And as soon as I do a little first aid on my nose we'll get right to it. You know I think you broke it. [*He is sticking pieces of kleenex up his nostrils.*]

ANNE Well I hope so. You frightened me half to death sneaking through my bedroom window like that.

POWER Yeah. Well you gave me a bit of a scare yourself. Do you always sleep in a fur coat. I thought you were a pack of dogs.

ANNE It was my mother's. I wear it when I need to be comforted. In times of stress. This is a very stress-filled time for me.

POWER Really. Tell me about it.

ANNE No. You had a chance earlier. You passed out. You had a second chance. Instead of meeting me, you sent someone to follow me.

POWER Give me a third and final chance. I'm at my best in clutch situations.

ANNE No. It's too late.

POWER Why?

ANNE Because Fred Whittacker is dead.

POWER Now how do you know that.

ANNE Stackhouse told me.

POWER Really ... But why should Whittacker's death mean anything to you.

ANNE Because he was the only one that could have helped me find Michael.

113

Nancy Beatty (ANNE) and David Bolt (T.M. POWER)

POWER So that you can protect him.

ANNE Right.

POWER Wrong! So that you could set him up for a hit by Pig Duvall.

ANNE Why would I want to do that.

POWER Because of your relationship with Duvall.

ANNE My relationship with Henry Duvall is none of your concern.

POWER Wrong again. It used to be none of my concern. Then Whittacker got killed. And I think it was my fault. You and your sister were spreading the word around that he was a blackmailer and I thought I could help him. I asked him to come here and somebody was waiting to kill him. That makes me responsible. That makes your relationship with Duvall and the Harrison family my concern.

ANNE I'm sorry your friend got killed. But in a sense it was his own fault. He was an extortionist.

POWER You know I'm having just one hell of a time believing that.

ANNE So you've heard the rumours.

POWER Which rumours?

ANNE The silly ones. The ones that say that Whittacker only took that money from Michael in order to give it to the campaigns of his two opponents. [*Pause.*]

POWER Yes. That's it. Now that makes sense. That's Whittacker. Good old Whittacker ... Damn him! Giving money away. Who does things like that.

ANNE Exactly. The whole idea is absurd.

POWER You say that because you've never met anyone like Whittacker. He hated everything Harrison stands for.

ANNE And what is that.

POWER Himself.

ANNE Nonsense. You've never met anyone like Michael. You can't believe that someone with his background could be anything but selfish or dishonest. It says more about how people like you form your ideas than anything else.

POWER He is dishonest. Whittacker had proof. Something worth half a million dollars.

ANNE All Whittacker found out was that Michael had been in a bit of trouble as a young man.

POWER What kind of trouble.

ANNE He was drunk. He beat up a young woman.

115

POWER Typical.

ANNE That kind of behaviour is not found exclusively in the upper classes Mr. Power. For example, the way you invaded my bedroom.

POWER Well who punched who in the nose, eh. Anyway, Harrison obviously didn't think it was such a small thing. He paid a lot of money to have it kept quiet.

ANNE He can afford the money. He couldn't afford the publicity. The election race is close. He wants it badly.

POWER That's what's wrong. Anyone who wants something that badly can't want it for the right reasons.

ANNE Please spare me your simple-minded ideology and your phony self-righteousness. If you really cared so much about those things you wouldn't be locked away in here would you.

POWER Oh, wouldn't I?

ANNE No.

POWER Look, this defence of Michael Harrison doesn't make sense. You can't have it both ways, Anne. You can't be on Michael's side and Duvall's at the same time. Not if what you wrote me in that letter is true. It doesn't make sense. Not even in your world where money *makes* everything make sense. How does Susan fit into all this.

ANNE Money this. Money that. Money. I am so tired of being insulted because I'm rich. My life is just as difficult as anyone's. More so.

POWER Really. Ah gee. That's tough, Anne.

ANNE What kind of world is this that a person has to apologize for being fortunate.

POWER A bad one. Tough luck. For all of us. Now I asked you, how does Susan fit into all this.

ANNE Leave my sister out of this.

POWER Why should I.

ANNE She's not ... I mean she ... she's been operating under a lot of stress lately.

POWER Sure. Operating under stress. Great work if you can get it. Is that why she got involved with a killer. And maybe even did a little killing on her own.

ANNE No! Look ... No. Forget it. I'll pay you a lot of money to forget everything.

POWER I don't want your money. I've got my own. I've become a
rich man. Independently wealthy.

ANNE Congratulations. Let's see how long *you* manage to
remain clean and innocent.

POWER Money doesn't corrupt everyone lady.

ANNE No. But it will sure as hell corrupt you. You've got too
many grudges. [*Pause.*]

POWER You're right.

ANNE Yes. Yes, I'm damn right.

POWER Shut up. You didn't know you were right. It was an
accident. You're just trying to confuse me to protect your
sister.

ANNE You're wrong.

POWER Prove it.

ANNE But –

POWER Prove it. Or I go after her with every bit of malice I can
muster.

ANNE It's just that I don't want her to be wrongly accused of
anything. I couldn't live with that. You see I ...

POWER Go on. [*Pause.*]

ANNE Well I did lie in that letter to you. I am involved with
Duvall. I don't know how, why, any of that. It just
happened. Funny, I can't remember how. Anyway I was
looking for Michael to help Duvall. To keep everything
Michael knew from hurting Duvall. Susan found out. And
was trying to get to Harrison before we did I guess. Susan
is innocent.... Leave her out of this.

POWER [*Looks at her. Goes and sits at his desk. And looks at her.
Long pause.*] Who killed Fred Whittacker.

ANNE I don't know.

POWER Duvall?

ANNE I don't know. Honestly.

POWER What's wrong. Doesn't he tell you how he spends his
spare time.

ANNE Please Mr. Power. I fell in love with him before I knew what
he was. I thought all that tough talk was just part of his
self-image. That he'd seen too many movies. How was I to
know he took it all seriously. Anyway it's difficult to stop
loving. I'm sure you know that.

POWER No. I don't. I don't know that. I don't know anything. [*He*

Steven Bush (HENRY)

puts his head on his desk. Pause. He lifts his head.] Nothing makes sense. Just like I always knew it wouldn't. Innocent people are getting killed because of other innocent people. Politicians are being assassinated by their fathers. Policemen are trying to prevent crimes only because they don't want to prosecute the people who commit them. And beautiful intelligent young women are falling in love with the scum of the earth.

ANNE   Please.

POWER   I can't help it Anne. You are a gross disappointment to me.

ANNE   You don't even know me.

POWER   [*drifting off*]. Well there was something in the way you looked. Even when I first saw you in that drunken haze. I don't know. Something. The kind of woman I usually make a fool of myself over. [*Pause.*]

ANNE   I guess that's a compliment.

POWER   Yeah I guess it is. [*Pause.*]

ANNE   You have a certain way about you yourself. It's not much. But it's obviously all yours.

POWER   I guess that's a compliment.

ANNE   More or less. [*Pause.*]

POWER   Well. [*Pause.*]

ANNE   Well ... [*Pause.* HENRY DUVALL *opens door, quickly. Stands at doorway. Long cold silence. All looking at each other.* DUVALL *motions for* ANNE *to leave.* ANNE *looks at* POWER. *Slowly leaves.* DUVALL *and* POWER *stare at each other.* DUVALL *looks over at aquarium. Looks at* POWER.]

DUVALL   Fish, eh? [*He smiles. Leaves. Pause.* POWER *goes to his filing cabinet. Unlocks a drawer. Takes out a gun in a shoulder holster. Puts on holster. Checks gun. Puts gun back in holster. The holster breaks from strap.* POWER *shakes his head. Throws holster on floor. Puts gun in his belt.*]

BLACKOUT

Scene Eight

Begins in darkness. Door opens. A bit of light spills in from hallway. Lights switched on. POWER *is standing by the door. Hand on the light switch.* HENRY DUVALL *is sitting at the desk, holding a gun pointed directly at* POWER.

POWER   Sorry. Wrong office. [*He flicks the switch. Darkness. A gun shot. Silence. Light.* DUVALL *is standing by the switch.* POWER *is gone.* DUVALL *looks around. Opens door. Looks up and down hallway. Searches office. Goes to window. Looks out. Turns back. An arm comes through the window and puts a gun to the back of* DUVALL's *head.* POWER *comes through the window.*]

POWER   Put that nasty weapon of yours down on the desk. [DUVALL *does so.*] You've got a touch of the cowboy in you, Duvall. You could have killed me.

DUVALL   If I'd wanted to. I didn't. I aimed high. Notice the bullet hole in the ceiling. [POWER *looks up.* DUVALL, *sensing this, pulls a fancy move. Whirls around and disarms* POWER. *Takes him by the collar and throws him against the wall.* POWER *crumples to the floor.* DUVALL *picks up his gun.*] Stand up. [*Pause.*] I said stand up.

POWER   I can't. I'm paralyzed from the waist down. Like all men I've had many nightmares about it and now it's really happened. You've seriously damaged my prospects for domestic happiness, Duvall.

DUVALL   Shut up. And get on your feet.

POWER   I can't.

DUVALL   You have two seconds.

POWER   [*Stands. Looks down at his legs.*] It's a miracle. Honestly. Two seconds ago I was a cripple and now without the benefit of medical science I can look forward once again to all those things which make life worth living. Getting arrested. Getting beat up. Getting shot at.

DUVALL   You talk a lot.

120

POWER Only when I'm tense. This kind of thing makes me tense. I'm sorry. I can't help it. Look at me Duvall. I'm tense. Very tense.

DUVALL Shut up.

POWER You've got to stop telling me to shut up. That makes me tense too.

DUVALL Maybe a whack across the back of your head would settle you down.

POWER Comments like that don't help either. They just reflect upon your own personality. Prove that you are a latent quasi-sexual full of self-hatred and a fear of women. Oh, I see that I've gone a bit too far and you are seriously considering blowing my stupid goddamn head off.

DUVALL You got it, Power.

POWER In that case let me suggest that all I need is a drink from a bottle of whiskey which is in my desk to calm my nerves and you will hear exactly what you want to hear from me from now on.

DUVALL Where in the desk.

POWER Upper right hand drawer.

DUVALL [*Turns. Opens drawer. Reaches in.* POWER *kicks the drawer shut on* DUVALL'*s hand. Wrestles the gun from* DUVALL'*s other hand. Points it at* DUVALL. *Steps back.* DUVALL *frees his hand from the drawer. Shakes it casually.*] For chrissake Power. I just wanted to talk. What is all this crap. I've got the gun. You've got the gun. I've got the gun.

POWER You left one out.

DUVALL What?

POWER It goes: You've got the gun, I've got the gun, you've got the gun, I've got the gun. See. I've got the gun.

DUVALL So what?

POWER Well it might not mean much to you but I feel much more comfortable this way. Now sit down. [DUVALL *obeys.*] Now talk.

DUVALL We want to make a deal.

POWER Who's 'we.'

DUVALL That's not important.

POWER You're right. What's the deal.

DUVALL You keep the money. We get the documents.

POWER What money. What documents.

DUVALL   Whittacker was carrying a briefcase with five hundred
         thousand dollars and a few pieces of paper in it. It wasn't
         turned in to the police.

POWER   You think I've got it.

DUVALL   Oh you've got it all right.

POWER   And why should I give it to you.

DUVALL   You don't listen! We just want the papers. You can keep
         the money.

POWER   Why can't I keep it all. Maybe I like the papers. Maybe
         they're fun to read. Maybe they provide a good education
         in civic politics.

DUVALL   [*Stands. Wanders over to aquarium. Is looking in.*] Maybe
         you'd like to use them to squeeze a whole lot more money
         out of ... someone.

POWER   Yeah. I've never had a lot of money before. It's gone to my
         head. I've become money mad. What's five hundred
         thousand dollars. Harrison has millions. Put that fish
         down!

DUVALL   [*Turns. Shows that his hands are empty. Smiles.*] How
         much do you want.

POWER   All of it.

DUVALL   How much do you think you'll get.

POWER   Another five hundred thousand. You see I want an even
         million. I want to be a millionaire. I want my mother to be
         able to tell her friends I made a million overnight. It
         sounds so good. Puts me in a class all my own. All those
         other jerks who say they made a million overnight really
         took four or five weeks. But I'm literally going to do it
         overnight. That gives you about five hours. Unmarked bills
         in small denominations in a plain brown briefcase.

DUVALL   And where are the documents?

POWER   They'll be here. Now get going. [DUVALL *stands.*] One more
         thing. My friend Jamie.

DUVALL   What about him.

POWER   He's missing. Do you know where he is.

DUVALL   Sure. I know where all the missing persons are. I'm their
         fucking patron saint.

POWER   Right. Well just in case, if anything happens to him, the
         documents go to the police. Get it?

DUVALL   Sure.

POWER   Now walk to the door.

DUVALL Sure. [*Obeys.*]

POWER Now get out of my sight as fast as possible.

DUVALL Sure. [*Smiles. Kicks the door off its hinges, propelling it into the hallway. Walks nonchalantly out of the office.*]

POWER [*Shakes his head. Pause.*] Typical quasi-sexual aggressiveness.

BLACKOUT

Scene Nine

Approximately four and a half hours later. POWER *is sitting on the floor counting money. He is taking it from the briefcase and dropping it into a garbage bag, one bill at a time. He is sad. The bottle of whiskey sits next to him. Empty. He is not drunk though. Just a bit tipsy. Down in the street a saxophone. Plaintive jazz. Very very well played.*

POWER Four hundred ninety-nine thousand, seven hundred. Four hundred ninety-nine thousand, eight hundred. Four hundred ninety-nine thousand, nine hundred. Four hundred ninety-nine thousand nine hundred and one. [*Picks up the last bill, looks at it, frowns.*] I've been robbed. [*Drops it.*] Ah well whoever it was, I forgive them. I forgive them all. I forgive petty malice. And unlimited greed. I forgive corruption and murder. I forgive the man who killed Fred Whittacker. And I forgive whoever it is who has been killing off all my family. [*Bows his head.*] Poor Aunt Sandra. Life. Do you know what life is. It's a bad smell. That's all. A bad smell. Ah what do you care Power. You're rich. You don't have to write your novel for another fifteen years just to give yourself something to do. You don't have to write articles on how professional architects spend their free afternoons. You don't have to live in this place without a door where people come in and say stupid things to you and make you do dangerous things for them. You're rich. You just have to keep your wits about you for the next little while and you can stay rich, be even richer. So rich you won't have to worry about these little

123

feelings of self-disgust you're having. Keep your wits about you, Tyrone. Stay rich. Self-disgust is a thing of the past. [*Someone is coming down the hall. Quickly* POWER *puts the garbage bag in amongst his other garbage bags.* JAMIE *comes in. Whistling. Kind of euphoric.*]

JAMIE What happened to the door.

POWER Someone kicked it in.

JAMIE Why.

POWER I don't know. I don't know anything. Life is too mysterious for me. I give up. [*Looks up.*] You're all right, eh.

JAMIE Sure. Why.

POWER Well I thought maybe ... Ah forget it.

JAMIE How do you like my new shirt. Susan gave it to me.

POWER New shirt, eh. [*Begins to cry.*]

JAMIE Are you drunk.

POWER No. [*Bows his head.*]

JAMIE What's wrong.

POWER What?

JAMIE You're crying.

POWER I'm just a little sad.

JAMIE Ah life's too short to be sad, Power. You're always sad.

POWER Self-disgust is a thing of the past. That's kind of sad in a funny sort of way. Take you for example. You went away with that woman and got drugged by deceit. You're disgusting. But you're not sad are you.

JAMIE [*smiles*]. No, I'm not.

POWER [*stands*]. When you get to be my age. And find yourself forgiving everything you detest that you've always detested then you'll be sad, I know. Because we're a lot alike.

JAMIE Oh no we're not.

POWER I've decided I have no morals. I'm giving up. Keeping the money. This is all too complex for me. I am pitiful. I really am.

JAMIE Power. Get a hold of yourself. You're depressing me. You're bringing me down.

POWER [*Shrugs. Groans.*] I just need some air. [*Goes over to window, leans out.*] Listen. He's playing so much better than he used to. He must have actually gone away and actually improved himself. That's ... that's wonderful.

That's sad. [*Starts to sob, turns, slumps into his chair, puts his head on the desk and continues to sob.*]

JAMIE   Tyrone. Tyrone. As soon as all this is over I'm going to get you the best psychiatrist money can buy.

POWER   [*Sits up suddenly. Angry.*] Money can't buy everything you know!! Did money make that saxophone player play better?!

JAMIE   Power. You have a split personality.

POWER   It's a sign of the times. Forget everything I've just said. We're starting over. I hereby dedicate the solution of this case to the memory of Fred Whittacker. Where's Susan.

JAMIE   I left her at home.

POWER   How long ago?

JAMIE   Half an hour.

POWER   All right. That should give her enough time.

JAMIE   For what.

POWER   No time for explanations. I made some phone calls earlier. Before I got drunk and decided to give up. We're expecting visitors. Henry Duvall is on his way here. [*Begins to tear his office apart. Emptying drawers, turning chairs over, etc.*]

JAMIE   You know, speaking of Susan. I got to know her pretty well in the last few hours. I think she was getting kind of fond of me. Things were happening.

POWER   Right. But you weren't the one who was making them happen.

JAMIE   I think we were falling in love or something.

POWER   Oh for chrissake. Bang your head against the wall, boy. Wake up. You were being used. She was using her sweet voice and her good looks on you.

JAMIE   Sure. I get it. What you're saying is a girl like her could see nothing in someone like me.

POWER   Exactly.

JAMIE   But she was –

POWER   Now don't bother me. I'm busy.

JAMIE   Yeah. I've noticed. What are you doing.

POWER   The forces of goodness have been here. The forces of justice. They smelled the rewards of evil and they came to snatch it away from me. I was lying unconscious on the floor and you came in and found me.

JAMIE   I don't get it.

POWER   [*Sits on the couch. Leans back. Rips his shirt.*] That's all you have to remember. I was lying unconscious on the floor and you came in and found me.

DUVALL   [*Comes in. Carrying briefcase.*] What happened!

JAMIE   He was lying unconscious on the floor and I came in and found him! [DUVALL *advances on* JAMIE. *Falsetto.*] Honest!

DUVALL   What happened!

POWER   It's gone. Someone hit me from behind, knocked me out and took it.

DUVALL   Bitch! [*He leaves.*]

POWER   [*Looks at* JAMIE. *Looks at doorway.*] It worked. It actually worked. [*Looks at* JAMIE.] We could have done without the [*in falsetto also*] honest!

JAMIE   Sorry. I was scared. He looked furious.

POWER   He was.

JAMIE   Why.

POWER   Because someone stole the incriminating papers from me.

JAMIE   Really?

POWER   No. But you should never tell the truth in the land of deception. You stick out like a sore thumb.

JAMIE   Why are you speaking in riddles.

POWER   Because I'm excited. My blood is boiling and my brain is working in strange and wondrous ways. Watch me Jamie, boy, I'm really quite a remarkable man. [ANNE SCOTT *appears in the doorway.*] Thank God you're here! [*He rushes to her.*] Henry Duvall has found out where Michael Harrison is hiding. He beat it out of me. And he's gone off to kill him.

ANNE   [*gets very upset*]. Oh no. Where is he.

POWER   In the basement of this building. I was hiding him for Whittacker.

ANNE   Call the police. I'll see if I can stop him. [*Runs off.*]

POWER   What do you think.

JAMIE   She was upset.

POWER   Not acting?

JAMIE   No way.

POWER   That's what I think too. How about that.

JAMIE   Very strange. I thought Duvall was her boyfriend.

POWER   No. Duvall is Susan's boyfriend.

JAMIE   Now wait a second, Power. I told you Susan was –

POWER   Shut up. We're using logic here. I realize it might be hard
on your animal instincts but it will save a lot of time.
Remember the process of elimination game? Remember
just now how Anne ran to protect Michael? Remember
the rumour that Duvall is involved with one of the Scott
sisters? Put all those things together with the fact that
Duvall is the bad guy and Michael Harrison is the closest
thing we've got to a good guy and you come up with the
fact that –

JAMIE   You come up with the fact that Anne wasn't on Duvall and
James Harrison's side. They were forcing her to help
them. That's what I saw in the livingroom at Harrison's.

POWER   Right. And if Anne wasn't on their side. Then what about
Susan.

SUSAN   [*Steps through the window from the fire escape. Holding a
gun with both hands.*] Susan was a bad girl.

POWER   And a liar. And a killer.

SUSAN   Where's Henry.

POWER   Looking for Anne.

SUSAN   Where's Anne.

POWER   Looking for Henry.

SUSAN   Oh aren't you clever Mr. Power.

POWER   Thank you. Tell me Susan. How did you get involved with
someone like Duvall. Did he have you on drugs or
something.

SUSAN   No. I found him exciting. I like exciting people.

POWER   Yeah, that's what I thought. [*To* JAMIE.] I just asked her the
question about drugs to be polite.

SUSAN   Where are the documents.

POWER   Be patient.

SUSAN   When Henry gets back he's going to be very upset with
you, Mr. Power.

JAMIE   If she was in with Duvall and Harrison why was she
pointing a gun at them in Harrison's window.

POWER   Duvall besides being 'exciting' is pretty smart I think.
Comes of years of sneaking around doing nasty things to

people. He knew we'd follow Anne from the bus station. You were to catch Susan pointing that gun and do just about what you did. It was a set-up. Throw suspicion on to Anne. Get Susan on our side. Find out where Michael Harrison was and put him out of his misery.

SUSAN Okay you've explained it all to stupid here, now where are the documents.

JAMIE Hey, don't call me stupid.

SUSAN Be quiet. Power, where are they.

POWER I don't know.

SUSAN I mean it. I'll blow your head off.

JAMIE No she won't.

SUSAN You stay where you are.

POWER Jamie.

JAMIE She won't do anything. Intuition. She's not a killer. I can tell. Duvall has her in some kind of trap or something. [*He is walking slowly toward her.*]

SUSAN I said stay where you are.

POWER Jamie.

JAMIE She won't – [*She fires.* JAMIE *clutches his chest. Drops to his knees.*] Power? [POWER *rushes to him.* JAMIE *dies in his arms.* SUSAN *has lowered her gun. She appears to be in shock.* STACKHOUSE *bursts through the door. Gun out.*]

STACKHOUSE Okay, Miss. Put it down. Drop it. [*She does.* STACKHOUSE *steps back into hallway. Reaches out with an arm and retrieves* DUVALL *who is handcuffed behind his back. Pushes him into room. Goes to* SUSAN. *Handcuffs her.*]

DUVALL You do that?

SUSAN Yes.

DUVALL Stupid.

SUSAN I thought it would be easy.

DUVALL Stupid.

STACKHOUSE Shut up. Both of you. Sit down. [*They do.*]

SUSAN You always said it was easy.

DUVALL Stupid.

STACKHOUSE Power. [*No response.*] Power.

POWER [*Has not moved. He is holding* JAMIE. *His head bowed.*] He's dead. [*He lets down* JAMIE's *body. Covers him with his jacket. Sits on the floor.*]

STACKHOUSE I got here just in time to catch Duvall taking off in his car just like you said. I arrested him. But I don't have anything on him. Power.

POWER Under the aquarium.

STACKHOUSE [*Retrieves the envelope from under the aquarium.*] What's this.

POWER Read it. And if you want more, I think he killed Whittacker. It was either him or his girlfriend.

STACKHOUSE Any proof?

POWER You find it. It's your job.

STACKHOUSE Yeah. [STACKHOUSE *gestures to* DUVALL *and* SUSAN.] You two. On your feet. Let's go. [*They start off.* DUVALL *stops.*]

DUVALL Hey Power. Aren't you going to tell him about the money you got from Whittacker. Aren't you going to be a good citizen, an honest man.

STACKHOUSE Well, Power?

POWER I don't have the money.

STACKHOUSE Are you sure you can live with that.

POWER I'll try.

DUVALL Welcome to my world, Mr. Power. Money wins. And I love it. Love watching it win. Just love it.

STACKHOUSE [*grabs his arm*]. Who asked you.

DUVALL I was expressing an opinion. [STACKHOUSE *pushes him.*] Don't push.

STACKHOUSE Sure. [*Pushes* DUVALL *again.*] Let's go. [STACKHOUSE, DUVALL, SUSAN *start off, meeting* ANNE SCOTT *at doorway. She looks at them, at* POWER *and* JAMIE. SUSAN *smiles at her.* STACKHOUSE, SUSAN *and* DUVALL *leave.* ANNE *walks slowly over to* POWER.]

ANNE Mr. Power. [*No response.*] Mr. Power.

POWER Your sister killed him. [ANNE *just lowers her head.*] I tried to tell him. Tried.

ANNE I'm sorry.

POWER Yeah. [*Pause.*] Michael Harrison is in a hotel in the west end. He'll come out of hiding now I guess.

ANNE Mr. Power I think I owe you an explanation.

POWER Forget it. I know. The older sister syndrome. Everything you did and said was to keep Susan from finding Michael and killing him.

ANNE Yes. I didn't want Michael to get hurt. But it was mostly to

129

POWER protect Susan. Habit I suppose. I've been doing it all my
life.

POWER The obvious becoming mysterious becoming disastrous.
Typical. You should have told me. It would have been
better.

STACKHOUSE [*comes back*]. Would you mind waiting downstairs for
me, Miss Scott, I have to ask you some questions.

ANNE All right. [*She starts off, stops.*] Mr. Power.

POWER Anne. Go away. [*She leaves.*]

STACKHOUSE Power.

POWER Go away. [*The telephone rings. Three times.* STACKHOUSE
answers it. POWER *goes and sits on the couch.*]

STACKHOUSE Yeah. Yeah it's me. Yeah that's all taken care of. [*Pause.*] I
know. I said I know! [*Pause.*] It's just that I don't much like
it. [*Pause.*] I understand that but I still don't like it, okay.
[*Pause.*] Yeah. But I don't know if he'll go for it. [*Pause.*]
Right ... Yeah. [*He hangs up. Long pause.*] Michael Harrison
will make a good mayor. That's what my employer wants.
That's probably what the people want too. He hasn't really
done anything wrong. Not really. I mean maybe he didn't
behave exactly courageously. But he wasn't – I mean ...
Look, what I'm saying is I need your guarantee that you'll
keep this whole thing quiet. [POWER *looks at him.*
STACKHOUSE *feels awkward. Wanders about the office. Goes
to the window.*] Listen to that guy down there. I had a hell
of a time getting those people into my car. He's attracted
quite a crowd. All the locals coming out to listen to him.
Quite a sight, really. I guess they've got nothing better to
do, eh. Saxophones. Jazz. Don't care for it myself. [*Long
pause.*] Power. I'll send some people to take care of ...
Power? [*No response.* STACKHOUSE *sticks his hands deeply
into his pockets. Walks out of the office.*

POWER [*Stands. Walks to aquarium. Feeds the fish. All this
aimlessly, almost trance-like. Walks to window. Looks out.
Walks over and retrieves the garbage bag with the money in
it. Walks to window. Climbs out. Starts to throw the money
down into the street. And screams.*] Don't vote for Michael
Harrison! Tell your friends! Tell everyone! Don't vote for
Michael Harrison! Don't vote for Michael Harrison! [*Lights

start to fade. Suddenly, JAMIE *sits up. Lights stop fading.*]

JAMIE Power! What the hell are you doing with my money?

[JAMIE *rushes to the window.* POWER *throws down the last of it. Steps into office.*]

POWER You're alive.

JAMIE Outa my way. I'm going down there.

POWER Too late. All gone.

JAMIE Where did you get the right to give away my share of that money!

POWER You were dead. I appointed myself the executor of your estate. What were you doing being dead.

JAMIE I was getting even with you. You set me up. You knew she was guilty and you left me alone with her. Right?

POWER [*shrugs*]. Sort of.

JAMIE Right. Well it was a pretty heartless thing to do. I could have been hurt. I thought you liked me. I thought I was the positive force in your life. Good thing for me I've got a talent for this business.... Sure I was soft on Susan. But something deep down inside said be careful.

POWER So you put blanks in her gun.

JAMIE Yeah.

POWER So where did you get them.

JAMIE I told you. I've got a talent for this business. Had you scared though didn't I.

POWER Oh don't be silly. I knew you weren't dead.

JAMIE You did not.

POWER No blood. Strong pulse. Chest moving in and out like a cow.

JAMIE You were too overcome by grief to notice those things.

POWER Overcome by grief. Give me a break.

JAMIE [*Walks to window. Shakes his head.*] You're a strange man, Power. Giving money away. Who does things like that. [*Walks back to* POWER.] The whole half million, Power? Didn't you keep any of it. Something to at least cover expenses.

POWER It was dirty. Very dirty. It had years of nasty stuff on it. You wouldn't have liked having it very much.

JAMIE Maybe. But I would have liked to make my own choice.

POWER Sorry. But you were dead. [*He smiles.*]

JAMIE   Oh shut up. [*He goes and sits down.*] Well it looks like we got nothing out of this. Nothing. And I even quit my job. How am I going to get through school without a job.

POWER   Get another.

JAMIE   If I can.

POWER   Quit school. Become a 'private eye.'

JAMIE   And turn out like you? No thanks.

POWER   What are you studying anyway. You never told me.

JAMIE   Political science.

POWER   [*laughs*]. You're kidding. Isn't that something. That's ... that's that's ... You know what life is. Life is –

JAMIE   Ah, who cares?

POWER   I do.

JAMIE   Well that's something at least.

POWER   Yeah.

JAMIE   Not much though.

POWER   No. [*They look at each other.*]

JAMIE   Not very goddamn much at all.

POWER   No.

JAMIE   [*Turns. Looks around the office. Long pause.*] You know what I think Power. I think we need a bigger office. [POWER *turns. Looks at him oddly.* JAMIE *looks back out window.*] Like the view though. [*A noise in the hallway.* JAMIE *goes out. Comes back carrying a piece of paper.*] Telegram.

POWER   Read it.

JAMIE   [*Reads it to himself.*] It's bad news.

POWER   Read it.

JAMIE   Your Uncle William is dead.

POWER   [*Bows his head. Goes slowly to his desk. Sits. Puts his head down. Long pause. Looks up.*] I don't have an Uncle William.

BLACKOUT

END

The Art of War

The Art of War was commissioned by Simon Fraser
University as the key-note address to the Conference on
Art and Reality, August 1982. It was first produced
professionally by Factory Theatre Lab, at Toronto
Workshop Productions, in February 1983, with the
following cast:

POWER. David Bolt
JAMIE. Jim Henshaw
HACKMAN. David Fox
BROWN. Dean Hawes
KARLA. Diane D'Aquila
HEATHER. Susan Purdy

Directed by George F. Walker
Stage managed by Peter Freund
Lighting and set designed by Jim Plaxton
Costumes designed by Miro Kinch
Score composed by John Roby

Persons in the Play
TYRONE M. POWER
JAMIE McLEAN
JOHN HACKMAN. *late forties*
BROWNIE BROWN, HACKMAN*'s aide; late forties*
KARLA MENDEZ, HACKMAN*'s guest*
HEATHER MASTERSON. *a local citizen*

The Place
In and around a large summer estate in Nova Scotia.
In the dead centre of summer.

*If an intermission is included, it should
occur between scenes Four and Five.*

Prologue

The murder of Paul Reinhardt.

Choreographed to heartbeat-rushing music.

Just before midnight at JOHN HACKMAN'*s summer estate. The house is a translucent glass bunker set into the side of a hill. We see a man looking in the front of the bunker. Then disappearing around the side. He is wearing an overcoat and a hat and he walks with a cane. The room is dimly lit, but we can make out a huge map of the world with flickering lights, some high-tech equipment and a few filing cabinets. The man enters from the side. Begins looking around. Takes out a camera and starts photographing everything. Looking through the files. In the distance we hear the voices of two men. Talking. Laughing. Getting closer. The man in the room hears them. Panics. Tries to tidy the room. Gives up. Tries to escape, but can't find an exit other than the one the voices seem to be near. Suddenly and simultaneously the two men are in the room. They are wearing evening clothes. The man in the overcoat throws himself with his arms out against the downstage wall of the bunker. It doesn't break and he remains splayed there. One of the men turns the lights in the room to full. The man in the overcoat tries to run between them. He is stopped. Thrown back. One of the men in evening clothes produces a long, thin knife. Advances. The man in the overcoat tries to rush out past him. He is stopped. Stabbed. Stabbed again. He falls. The men in evening clothes look at each other. Then one turns away.*

BLACKOUT

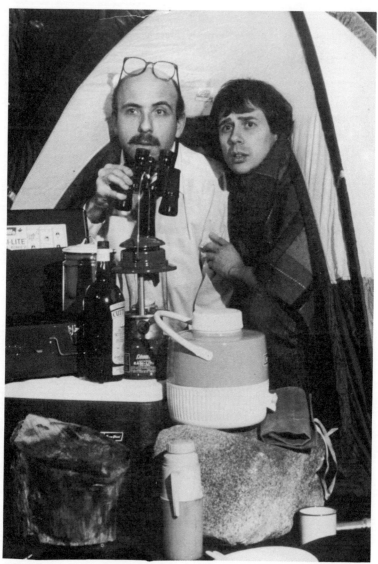

David Bolt (T.M. POWER) and Jim Henshaw (JAMIE)

Scene One

Midnight. The beach. Two figures approaching. HACKMAN *is carrying a flashlight.* BROWN *is carrying a corpse wrapped in a blanket over his shoulder.*

HACKMAN Is he heavy, Brown?

BROWN No, sir. Light as a feather. A burden of love.

HACKMAN Anywhere around here should do. Put him down. [BROWN *drops the corpse.* HACKMAN *starts to dig.*]

BROWN I'll do that, sir. You'll get yourself covered in sand.

HACKMAN Thank you, Brown. [*Hands* BROWN *the shovel.* BROWN *starts to dig.*] It's a lovely night, isn't it.

BROWN Yes, sir. Shame to waste it in the company of strangers.

HACKMAN Oh he's no stranger, Brown. He's the enemy.

BROWN He *was* the enemy ... And not a very good one if I may say so, sir.

HACKMAN You killed him well, Brown. He didn't have a chance.

BROWN Thank you, sir.

HACKMAN Reminded me of the killing you used to do in the old days.

BROWN Afraid I'm a little out of practice. Had to stick it in twice.

HACKMAN Well perhaps you rushed it a bit. Didn't take time to appreciate the act fully. Nevertheless, it was an exciting thing to watch. It had an artistic touch. You're a bit of an artist in your own way, did you know that Brown.

BROWN Never thought of it that way, sir.

HACKMAN You can you know, from now on, if you want.

BROWN I'm not much on art and artists, sir.

HACKMAN Well it's all how you look at it. I suppose I'll be meeting a lot of artists in my new job. Most of them won't be very good I imagine. This dead man was an artist of sorts. A writer.

BROWN How deep do you want this, sir?

HACKMAN Oh not too deep. I don't suppose anyone will be looking for him. Yes. It's a lovely night. Stop for a moment, Brown. Look at it. The night.

137

BROWN [*Stops. Looks around vacantly. Then looks at the corpse.
Smiles.*] Why you're right, sir. It is.

HACKMAN You see, Brown. You just have to take the time to
appreciate things. A lovely night. A lovely killing. [BROWN
starts to dig.]
BLACKOUT

Scene Two

Dawn. On a nearby cliff. POWER *and* JAMIE. POWER *is looking
down through a pair of binoculars.* JAMIE *is sitting on the
grass, chin in his palms. There is a pile of camping gear
nearby.*

POWER *is middle-aged. Balding. With a walrus mustache.
Glasses. Wearing an overcoat.* JAMIE *is in his early twenties.
Sort of wiry. In jeans and a sweater.*

JAMIE What are you doing.

POWER Looking for signs of strange behaviour.

JAMIE Well you can look at us, Power. I'd say our behaviour is
pretty strange. Sitting on top of a cliff a thousand miles
from home at five o'clock in the morning.

POWER The guy who lives down there is a maniac.

JAMIE You seem to be developing an obsession with him. Why?

POWER He's a maniac. Whatya mean, obsession. I'm not obsessed.
He's up to something, that's all. Something vile and
dangerous I'll bet. He needs to be watched.

JAMIE Then maybe we should tell the authorities.

POWER 'Authorities'?! You make it sound like an agency of the
Lord or something. This guy down there, this John C.
Hackman, retired general, is the authority. He's an adviser
to a goddamn cabinet minister in the goddamn
government. And he's a maniac. When he was advisor to
the Minister of Defence he was suspected of cooking up
bizarre arms deals with lunatic Third World politicos and
military types.

JAMIE That's why he was fired?

POWER He wasn't fired. They just got him off the front pages. They
shuffled him over to the Minister of Culture.

Scene Two

JAMIE I didn't know we had a Minister of Culture. What does he do.

POWER It's a secret. I'm not even sure the Minister of Culture knows. It's not exactly a high-priority position. And just to prove it they make Hackman his special adviser. The guy is a career soldier. His idea of a cultural event is bombing an opera house.

JAMIE I think your bias is screwing up your judgement, as usual. I haven't noticed anything strange about him.

POWER You've only been working for him for a week. He's being cautious around you. Checking out your references. Did you take care of your references.

JAMIE No problem.

POWER Be more specific.

JAMIE When they check they'll find that I've been a gardener at some of the best homes in the area.

POWER How did you manage that.

JAMIE As one private detective to another, it took some doin' but it was done.

POWER Look. How many times do I have to tell you. We're not private detectives. I'm just a concerned citizen. And you're a punk who follows me around.

JAMIE Well at least I'm a punk with a job. Good thing my cover on this one is to be gainfully employed because I'm starting to get the impression we don't have a client. We stand to make zippo on this case. Unless your friend Reinhardt is going to pay us.

POWER Reinhardt is dead. Hackman killed him.

JAMIE You know this for sure.

POWER I sense it for sure.

JAMIE All you know is he hasn't come home.

POWER He told me he was coming down here because he had a tip that Hackman was up to something. Reinhardt was the kind to dig in. He'd go right into the belly of the mess and all its danger. He wasn't subtle, but he was a good newspaperman.

JAMIE Oh Jesus. You knew this guy Reinhardt when you were a reporter. You didn't tell me that. Is he your age.

POWER Just about. Why.

JAMIE For chrissake, Power. He's probably a disillusioned paranoid drunk just like you were when I met you.

POWER Shut up.

JAMIE You're all the same. That generation of yours. Scandals in every corner. Corruption on every level. I'm going home. If Reinhardt is dead, he died of alcohol poisoning.

POWER Reinhardt didn't drink. He was a whatyacallit.

JAMIE A junkie?

POWER Shut up. He was Born Again.

JAMIE Yeah. Well I was only born once but it wasn't yesterday. And I'm not putting my life in jeopardy under these increasingly dubious circumstances. You led me to believe this was a simple job of observation and that there was a lot of money to be made.

POWER Because that's the only way I can get you to do anything. By talking about financial profit. You're a greedy money-grabbing amoral smart-ass.

JAMIE And you're a cause in search of an issue. Life is precious, Power. I don't want to waste it trying to reconstruct your social conscience.

POWER The quality of life is precious. Life itself is meaningless.

JAMIE Quality is defined by quantity. Money buys you both.

POWER No. Money is just –

JAMIE I don't want to talk about this on this goddamn cliff at five o'clock in the morning!

POWER Fine. We won't. We'll just do our jobs. You will report back to work at Hackman's and keep your eyes and ears open and I'll continue my investigation.

JAMIE Why.

POWER Why for me. Or why for you.

JAMIE Just why.

POWER Why for me is I think Hackman is up to something evil, dangerous, and destructive. Why for you is because you're the smart-ass punk who has been following me around for a year and a half and is now going to do something to pay me back for letting you do it.

JAMIE Wrong. Why for me is I'm learning a trade. Because realize it or not you're not the useless investigative reporter you used to be. You've become a pretty fair private detective and I'm your partner.

POWER All right. Look at life in your own strange brittle romantic way. You're a hard case. Just do your job. And when I show up at Hackman's try to avoid recognizing me.

JAMIE   How are you going to get in there.

POWER   I think I've got a contact in the town who can help me. I'm meeting her for breakfast. I've got to get going.

JAMIE   Why so early.

POWER   Because it's five miles and I have to walk.

JAMIE   Why didn't you rent a car.

POWER   With what. I spent almost everything I had on my camping gear.

JAMIE   We're pitiful. We're pathetic. We're poor. And why. Because you take these cases where there's no money involved.

POWER   I'm poor because I'm a freelance writer with diminishing talent. You're poor because you don't work. You just follow me around. Reality, boy. Try it out. Goodbye. [*Starts off, stops.*] Do me a favour. Throw my tent.

JAMIE   Where.

POWER   Right where it is.

JAMIE   Oh you mean put it up.

POWER   That's what I said.

JAMIE   The expression is 'pitch the tent,' Power. Not 'throw it.' Your grasp of contemporary idiom is scary.

POWER   Goodbye. [*Leaves.* JAMIE *starts to unpack the camping gear.*]

JAMIE   'Reality, boy. Try it out.' The man's in middle-age standing on top of a cliff talking about politicians and Third World lunatics and the quality of life and he worries about my sense of reality. He's gotta be kidding. What's this. [*From inside a duffle-bag he produces a rifle with a telescopic sight on it.*] He's gotta be kidding. Seriously.

BLACKOUT

Scene Three

Midday. The patio and garden of HACKMAN's *house.*
HACKMAN, *in shirtsleeves, is sitting in a lawn chair reading a newspaper.*

KARLA MENDEZ *is pacing. She is a tall, dark, angular woman in her late thirties. Tastefully, simply dressed. Wearing dark glasses. She speaks with a slight accent.*

KARLA The phone is not ringing.

HACKMAN Be patient.

KARLA He was to call at noon. It is now noon plus twenty.

HACKMAN He'll call.

KARLA I think something has happened. At the airport. It always happens at the airport.

HACKMAN You worry too much. His papers are in order. I arranged them myself.

KARLA You are not God.

HACKMAN I never said I was.

KARLA You speak sometimes like God. 'I did *that*. So this is what will happen.' 'I made this arrangement so it is all right.' Only God can make these assurances and you are not God. You are only a politician. You work for the 'minister of culture.' [*Laughs abruptly.*]

HACKMAN How many more jokes are you going to make about that.

KARLA I think it is funny. I think it is ridiculous.

HACKMAN Ridiculous enough to be out of the limelight. But not too ridiculous to keep the connections that allow me to make certain arrangements.

KARLA We'll see. If he calls. We'll see.

HACKMAN Stop pacing.

KARLA I'm making you nervous?

HACKMAN It's annoying.

KARLA Do I care. Did I ask to be sent here.

HACKMAN I thought you did. I thought you wanted to be close to me.

KARLA I have not wanted to be close to you for over three years. Being close to you is being close to disappointment.

HACKMAN Remember the month we spent together in Panama City?

KARLA No. See? I am over you. I even have no memory of you.

HACKMAN In Panama City you were not disappointed.

KARLA You misunderstand what I mean by disappointment. You misunderstand what I mean by everything. I should have taken my father's advice about you.

HACKMAN What did he say.

KARLA He said 'Keep it strictly business with that man. He is good for business. Bad for everything else.'

HACKMAN Your father is a great man and he will be a great leader for

142

your people but about things that concern you he has no judgement. He's just a father.

KARLA   Nevertheless. You soon proved him right. Several times in fact.

HACKMAN   Fidelity. That's what this is about. Loyalty to you.

KARLA   Or to anything. [*Checks her watch.*] Call the airport. Perhaps the flight is delayed.

HACKMAN   If it's delayed, it's delayed. Be patient. He'll call. [JAMIE *comes on, walking by, pushing a wheelbarrow full of rocks.*] You. Stop. Excuse me, what's your name again?

JAMIE   Jamie. Jamie McLean.

HACKMAN   Yes. Well, Jamie. Would you mind telling me what you're doing.

JAMIE   Taking these rocks over to that flower bed.

HACKMAN   Aren't those the same rocks you removed from that flower bed yesterday.

JAMIE   No, sir. These are the rocks I took from around the shrubs out front and put around the rose bushes at the side. The rocks I took from that flower bed I put around the shrubs out front. You're probably wondering what rocks I'm going to put back around the rose bushes now that these are gone.

HACKMAN   No, I'm wondering why, since you've been employed as my gardener for over a week, all you've done is move rocks around.

JAMIE   It's my personal concept in gardening. Work from the outside in. Get the look of it before you deal with the substance.

KARLA   Typically North American.

HACKMAN   Some of the roses are dying.

JAMIE   Don't worry about it, sir. They'll be all right as soon as I get the right rocks in place. Roses are sensitive. They know they're not yet properly showcased.

HACKMAN   You're not a flake are you, Jamie. You talk like a flake.

JAMIE   Trust me, sir.

HACKMAN   You come highly recommended. But you talk like a flake and you seem to be obsessed with rocks.

JAMIE   Trust me, sir. I'm an innovator.

HACKMAN   See that's what I mean. 'I'm an innovator.' What kind of thing is that for a gardener to say.

JAMIE   Sorry. Would you prefer I kept my conversation more rustic.

KARLA   Really, John. So much fuss over a bunch of flowers.

HACKMAN   I'm very fond of my garden! It's a kind of passion. [*The phone rings. It is on a small table next to* HACKMAN. *He answers it. On phone.*] Yes ... Good ... Yes ... Goodbye. [*Hangs up; to* KARLA.] He's here. You should leave. He's expecting you.

KARLA   Where.

HACKMAN   The airport.

KARLA   The airport?

HACKMAN   Yes. [*To* JAMIE.] Excuse me.

JAMIE   Yeah.

HACKMAN   Why are you standing there.

JAMIE   Awaiting further instructions, sir. Are there any.

HACKMAN   Yes. Stop messing around with rocks. And take care of my garden. I love my garden! Understand?

JAMIE   [*gulps*]. You bet. Goodbye ma'am. Goodbye, sir [*Goes off, leaving the wheelbarrow.*]

HACKMAN   Yes. The airport.

KARLA   Dangerous.

HACKMAN   It's arranged. I'm having him watched. I don't want him leaving there. He'll be too hard to follow.

KARLA   I don't like doing this kind of business in public places.

HACKMAN   Just go. It's arranged.

KARLA   You go.

HACKMAN   He won't talk to me. It has to be you. That's why you were sent here. Now go. [KARLA *stares at him for a moment. Then starts off.*] Oh Karla.

KARLA   What.

HACKMAN   [*Reaches under his lawn chair. Produces an attaché case.*] It's money. He'll want money.

KARLA   No he won't.

HACKMAN   He's doing this for money, Karla.

KARLA   I don't believe that. He's doing it out of loyalty to my father.

HACKMAN   Well if you're absolutely sure, don't take it. [KARLA *mutters an obscenity. She grabs the attaché case. Leaves.* HACKMAN *returns to his newspaper.* JAMIE *comes back on sheepishly. Starts to push wheelbarrow off quietly.* HACKMAN *peers over his newspaper.* JAMIE *catches his eye.*]

144

JAMIE   I don't have any plans for these rocks, sir. It's just that I
        need the wheelbarrow for ... for ... dirt.

HACKMAN   Dirt?

JAMIE   Soil. [HACKMAN *disappears behind the newspaper.* JAMIE
        leaves. Shaking his head. BROWN *comes on. In a crisp
        business suit.*]

BROWN   Heather Masterson is here to see you.

HACKMAN   Send her away.

BROWN   She claims to have an appointment.

HACKMAN   She's lying. I'm on vacation. This is my summer residence.
        I don't make appointments here.

BROWN   You do when you are very drunk, sir. You were at a party
        together last Wednesday night. You probably made the
        appointment then.

HACKMAN   Let her in. [BROWN *goes off.* JAMIE *comes on carrying a small
        bush. Whistling. Crosses in front of* HACKMAN. HACKMAN
        watches him leave. HEATHER MASTERSON *and* POWER *come
        out of the house onto the patio. She is in her late twenties.
        Preppy.* POWER *is in shirtsleeves. His coat thrown over his
        shoulder. Hands in his pockets. Sweating.*]

HEATHER   Good morning, General.

HACKMAN   Hello.

HEATHER   I'm glad you remembered I was coming. I was afraid you
        wouldn't. [*To* POWER.] The General came to my birthday
        party last week. He and my daddy are old friends. My
        daddy got him a little bit loaded and I decided to take the
        opportunity to bamboozle an official appointment. [*To*
        HACKMAN]. Oh, I'm sorry. This is Mr. Power. He was just
        dying to meet you and I didn't think you'd mind. Do you
        mind?

HACKMAN   I'm not sure. [*Looks* POWER *over. Then extends a hand. They
        shake.*] Mr. Power.

POWER   General. I've followed your career for many years.

HACKMAN   Idle curiosity?

HEATHER   Mr. Power is a writer.

HACKMAN   Really. Of what?

HEATHER   Oh you can talk to him in a minute. I've got the official
        appointment, remember.

HACKMAN   Very well. Would you like to sit down.

HEATHER   No thanks.

145

POWER   I will if you don't mind. I had a long walk this morning. And I think I'm dying. [*Sits in a lawn chair.*]

HEATHER   You're about twenty pounds overweight.

POWER   It's the fresh air. They say it's like poison if you're not used to it.

HEATHER   A man your age has to be careful. My daddy is careful.

POWER   Your daddy is rich. He can afford to be careful. I'm poor. I have to take chances.

HEATHER   I didn't get that. [*To* HACKMAN.] did you?

HACKMAN   Heather. I thought you had something to ask me. I've got a busy day ahead of me.

HEATHER   Right. Sorry. Well as you know I am a member of the local historical board. It's great. It's local. It's historical. [POWER *looks at her.*] And we have been trying unsuccessfully for two years to open our own museum. So when we found out that you had been made an adviser to the Minister of Culture we were sure you could –

HACKMAN   Excuse me. [*Picks up his phone, buzzes.*] Brownie, get out here. [*Hangs up.*] This might save us both some time. [BROWN *comes out.*] Do we have anything to do with the allocation of funds to museums.

BROWN   No sir. Minister of Education handles that.

HACKMAN   Sorry, Heather.

HEATHER   But surely the Minister of Culture –

HACKMAN   Heather. It's a new position. Just created. We don't know exactly what it means yet ourselves. [*Laughs.*]

POWER   When will you.

HACKMAN   I beg your pardon.

POWER   When can we expect an official statement of the Minister's responsibilities.

HACKMAN   You asked that question like a journalist, Mr. Power.

POWER   Is that good.

HEATHER   Listen, General, I promised the Historical Board that you would help.

HACKMAN   Heather. That conversation is over.

HEATHER   Well that really pisses me off. You didn't even listen, and that really is a piss-off! I'm leaving! I mean it. [*Pause, no response. She starts off.*] I'll wait for you in the car Mr. Power. [*She leaves.* BROWN *starts to follow her.* HACKMAN

146

Scene Three

signals him to stay. BROWN *stands beside* HACKMAN. *Arms folded.*]

HACKMAN The name Power sounds familiar ... [BROWN *whispers in* HACKMAN*'s ear.* HACKMAN *smiles.*] There was a T.M. Power who used to write a syndicated political column. Is that you?

POWER Yes.

HACKMAN I hated every word you wrote.

POWER In my own way, so did I.

HACKMAN Hated with a passion. Hated all journalism. Hated the media in general. Of course that was when I was adviser to the Minister of Defense. Now that I'm working for the Minister of Culture I have a different attitude.

POWER You just don't give a damn. Politically speaking, I mean.

HACKMAN The Minister of Culture officially supports the power of the written word. And the spoken word.

POWER What about song lyrics.

HACKMAN [*smiles*]. Oh, he has a Deputy Minister that handles music. I'm afraid the Minister is a bit of an ignoramus in that area.

POWER Please don't apologize for him. I mean think about it. There are only twelve notes. Musicians just move them around. What's all the fuss.

HACKMAN I get the feeling you sometimes speak to hear your own voice, Mr. Power.

POWER It's a habit I got into when I was covering the capital. Talking to politicians. There was nothing coming my way. I had to compensate.

HACKMAN Why did you want to meet me.

POWER I'm working freelance now. I'm fishing around for something to write about.

HACKMAN You think the creation of a minister of culture is a joke.

POWER Don't you?

HACKMAN What do you know about me.

POWER You're a soldier.

HACKMAN I was a soldier.

POWER Some old soldiers never die. They just start pan-American right-wing organizations.

HACKMAN That of course is an old and unfounded rumour.

147

POWER   Then why were you moved off the defence portfolio.

HACKMAN I wanted a change. A chance for a middle-aged man to develop a new passion.

POWER   Come off it, General. Men like you have room for only one passion in their lives. And yours is not art and culture.

HACKMAN What is it then.

POWER   Oh God. Well let's simplify it. Let's call it the communist menace.

HACKMAN [*groans*]. And you don't believe in the communist menace.

POWER   Actually I do. The communist menace. And the fascist menace. The menace of the church. The menace of channelled information. The menace of ignorance. The menace of indifference. The menace of war. I'm sort of a menace specialist.

HACKMAN No. You're just a liberal.

POWER   What's that supposed to mean.

HACKMAN You think the human race is going on a journey. To peace and enlightenment. And that it's a journey everyone has the ability and the right to make.

POWER   And you don't.

HACKMAN Let's just say I don't insist upon it. And another thing. You probably have an unholy fear of something which I take more or less for granted.

POWER   What.

HACKMAN The vast darkness. [BROWN *looks at* POWER. *Smiles.*]

POWER   The vast darkness. The existential version?

HACKMAN No, let's simplify it. Let's call it war. The new war. The inevitable destruction of everything. Life-ending war. But even without war, it ends. Everything we build now will be ruins in, what, a thousand years, anyway. [*Looks at* BROWN. BROWN *gestures a shrug with his hand.*] War is a way of taking temporary control, that's all. Try thinking about war that way and it won't scare you so much. Something wrong?

POWER   [*Rubbing his forehead.*] I've suddenly developed one hell of a headache. [HACKMAN *signals* BROWN.]

BROWN   Sir, it's getting late. You have several letters to dictate. And a telephone call to make. Miss Masterson is waiting in the car for this gentleman. And also ... also ... [*Rubs his head.*]

HACKMAN [*checks his watch*]. I didn't realize it was getting so late.

POWER   Time flies when you're talking about fun stuff. [BROWN *is rubbing his head furiously.*]

HACKMAN   Are you all right, Brownie.

BROWN   Sir. In a minute sir.

POWER   What's wrong with him.

BROWN   [*advancing*]. War wound!

HACKMAN   Quite serious when it flares up.

POWER   Sorry to hear that. [*Rubs his own forehead. Stands.*]

HACKMAN   [*puts his arm around* POWER]. Look, Mr. Power, if you're going to be around for a few days perhaps we could talk again. Actually I'd like to insist upon it. If you're going to write anything about me, I'd like a chance to balance some of your preconceptions. Next time we'll talk about art not war. You'll see that there's more to me than most people think.

POWER   Oh I'm sure of that.

HACKMAN   I really want to make the Department of Culture work. You could say I'm like anyone else who's new on the job and anxious to make a good impression. How can I reach you.

POWER   Through Heather.

HACKMAN   You're staying with the Mastersons?

POWER   No. But I'll be contacting her.

HACKMAN   Then where are you staying.

POWER   Around. Here and there.

HACKMAN   Why so secretive?

POWER   Habit. [*Frees himself from* HACKMAN. *Starts off. Stops.*] By the way. How did you get on with Paul Reinhardt.

HACKMAN   I'm sorry. I don't know what you mean. Who is he.

POWER   A journalist friend of mine. He was coming down here to interview you. Never showed up, eh?

HACKMAN   Not as far as I know. Brownie?

BROWN   No, sir.

POWER   Odd. [*Rubs his head.*]

HACKMAN   How bad is that headache.

POWER   I'll live.

HACKMAN   That's it. Think positively.

BROWN   I'll show you out. [*Rubs his forehead again.*]

POWER   No thanks. I can find my own way. You better get some rest. [BROWN *just looks at him.* POWER *leaves.*]

HACKMAN   Three things. Find out what he's been up to since he stopped writing that ridiculous column. Find out what his connection is to Heather Masterson. Find out what he and our late friend Paul Reinhardt had in common besides the fact that they were both bad writers. [JAMIE *walks by carrying a bunch of flowers.*] What are you doing with those flowers.

JAMIE It's a surprise, sir. [*Leaves.*]

HACKMAN One more thing. Check that kid's references out again. He's murdering my garden. I love that garden!
BLACKOUT

Scene Four

Late evening. On the cliff. The tent is up. The area is lit by a gas lantern placed on a camping-stool. POWER *is lying unconscious on his sleeping bag, half in and half out of the tent. An empty liquor bottle beside him. Sound of someone approaching.* JAMIE *comes on, cautiously.*

JAMIE Power? Power, it's me. Don't shoot. [*Sees* POWER.] Tyrone. [*Goes to him.*] He's dead. [*Bends down.*] He's dead drunk. I knew it would come to this. The man has no self-discipline. He is doomed to a life of self-abuse. [*Shakes* POWER.] Power. Power, wake up, you're disgusting. [POWER *whimpers, twitches.*] Don't whimper. It's really pitiful when you whimper. Wake up. [*Shakes him.*]

POWER [*Raises an arm. Speaks just above a whisper.*] Leave me alone.

JAMIE Wake up!

POWER Leave me alone. Please! [*Whimpers.*]

JAMIE Stop whimpering! [*Shakes him violently.* POWER *sits up suddenly.*] What's going on?! [JAMIE *stands. Moves away.*] What were you doing. Trying to pick my pocket? Looking for loose change?

JAMIE You were having a bad dream. I thought I'd better wake you up.

150

POWER   What time is it. I must have dozed off.

JAMIE   Give me a break. You were drunk. You passed out. I thought you were through with the booze. Don't you know how disgusting you are when you drink.

POWER   A temporary relapse.

JAMIE   How many times do I have to tell you. You're an alcoholic. You have a serious drinking problem.

POWER   [*Getting up slowly.*] No, you have a serious drinking problem. A man has a few sips and you get all sweaty and start sermonizing. You have an unnatural fear that anyone who touches liquor will turn out like your father.

JAMIE   Leave my father out of this.

POWER   Look, Jamie. All I'm saying is that I'm not a common drunk like he was. [*Pouring himself a coffee from a thermos.*]

JAMIE   Oh no. Not you. You drink for the pain in the universe and the soul of mankind. You're not a common drunk. You're a common pretentious drunk.

POWER   It was Hackman. He drove me to it.

JAMIE   Power. I was eavesdropping. I overheard your entire conversation. He sounded perfectly rational. You sounded perfectly obnoxious.

POWER   He drove me to being obnoxious. His kind always does. A knee-jerk reaction. What do you mean he sounded rational. Didn't you hear him talking about the vast darkness.

JAMIE   He was egging you on. It was a joke.

POWER   It was no joke. It was his definition of reality. He was speaking from the heart of his moral code.

JAMIE   I didn't understand a word of it.

POWER   That's because you don't have a moral code of your own to cross-reference with. He was speaking from the heart of his moral code and the heart of my moral code picked up the signals and got very, very depressed.

JAMIE   And made you go out and buy a bottle of scotch.

POWER   No. I had it with me. I had a feeling I might need it before we were through.

JAMIE   Yeah. Well, anticipation is the better part of cowardice.

POWER   I'm not afraid of him. He just depresses me.

JAMIE   Oh yeah? [*Picks up the duffle bag and takes out the rifle.*]

151

Well if you're not afraid of him what are you doing with this.

POWER He killed Reinhardt. I know he killed him. I had a feeling about it when I was there. A kind of mental picture. And he's up to something!

JAMIE Are you going to shoot him down, Power.

POWER Someone has to shoot him down.

JAMIE What?

POWER I was speaking metaphorically.

JAMIE Oh, so this is a metaphor. It's not a rifle. And you're not going to shoot him because you're not afraid of him even though you saw him kill your friend Reinhardt in one of your moments of psychic clarity because he's up to something which is vaguely concerned with some lunatic Third World politico and you want to find out what it is. Or maybe you don't want to find out what it is. You just want to create a mental metaphor for what it is. Then why do you have this *fucking rifle*!

POWER Because he's dangerous!

JAMIE And you're afraid of him!

POWER Yes!

JAMIE Thank you. I thank you. All of us who desperately believe in holding on to reality thank you. [*Pause.*] Power?

POWER What?

JAMIE I'm afraid of him too.

POWER Why. What did he say.

JAMIE It's not what he says. It's how he says it. And it's who he hangs around with. That guy Brown.

POWER Killer eyes.

JAMIE Yeah. You noticed them, eh. He's an ex-commando. A sergeant-major.

POWER How'd you find that out.

JAMIE He told me.

POWER Exchanging pleasantries?

JAMIE I think it was a threat. There's a room in that house full of filing cabinets and high-tech machinery that I'm not even allowed to go near. It was his way of explaining why it's not guarded. Sort of a challenge. 'I'm an ex-commando and you're a skinny little kid. You want to try sneaking in that room late at night you better bring an army.' I got the

message. So, Power, if you're going to suggest I do some
after-hours snooping, don't.

POWER Off-limits, eh. Private chambers, eh. What did I tell you. A
nefarious sneaky dangerous vile disgusting plot!

JAMIE Calm down. Maybe it's just where he keeps his love
letters.

POWER Love? Him? Mr. Vast Darkness. I can't imagine him having
sex. Unless he's drilled a hole in an ICBM.

JAMIE There is a lady. She's staying there.

POWER What's her name.

JAMIE Karla.

POWER Her last name.

JAMIE Don't know.

POWER What's she look like.

JAMIE Terrific.

POWER Be a little more specific.

JAMIE Tall. Dark. Intense. Terrific.

POWER Did she have an accent.

JAMIE Sort of.

POWER What kind.

JAMIE Foreign.

POWER You've got a mind like a computer.

JAMIE I meant foreign in a general way. As a way of saying I
couldn't pinpoint it.

POWER Mendez. Karla Mendez. It could be her. And you think
they're lovers?

JAMIE Well there was something going on between them. I could
sense it. It was kind of exciting. He's different with her. Still
dangerous but also kind of warm somehow.

POWER Shut up. You're making me sick.

JAMIE Sure. I know. I'm sensitive to those things in a way you're
not. You're good at sensing paranoid things like death and
misery. That's why you won't live long. That's why you're
a disgusting drunk.

POWER And you're a romantic fool. Put any man and any woman
together and you have a delirious feeling of self-
projection. Have you asked her to walk on your face yet.

JAMIE You hate women, don't you.

POWER Look. Crawl out of my subconscious, will you. Why are
you always saying things like that to me.

JAMIE   Because you've never had a successful romance and I think that has a lot to do with your problems. Besides, you started it.

POWER   I was just trying to bring you back to earth. You were falling in love with Karla Mendez or at least falling in love with the idea of falling in love which is more your style, and that could be very dangerous.

JAMIE   Why.

POWER   She's a terrorist. And a fascist. The daughter of a supreme fascist. A killer. Her father's in prison and she's wanted all over the world.

JAMIE   Sure. And she's sitting down there casually as a guest of Hackman's.

POWER   Why not? Who could see her.

JAMIE   Me. I saw her.

POWER   But you're just a gardener.

JAMIE   Yeah. But even so –

POWER   Shush. Someone's coming. [*Someone is.*] Quick. The rifle. Pick it up.

JAMIE   You pick it up.

POWER   Pick it up and point it.

JAMIE   It's your rifle. You pick it up.

POWER   I hate guns. You know I hate guns. You're the one who loves guns. Now pick it up. Someone's out there.

JAMIE   I don't love guns.

POWER   Oh you do so. You love them. Playing with them. Talking about them. Being a private eye. Being tough. Using force. Except now when we might be killed. Now pick up that goddamn rifle!!

JAMIE   All right! [*Picks it up.* POWER *gets behind* JAMIE.]

POWER   Who's out there.

HEATHER   [*appears from behind the tent*]. It's just me.

POWER   Oh, hello. What are you doing out here so late.

HEATHER   Tyrone, would you mind asking your friend to lower the rifle.

POWER   It's okay, Jamie ... Jamie. [*But* JAMIE *is in love. He is smiling like a moron.* POWER *looks at* JAMIE. *Looks at* HEATHER. *At* JAMIE. *Shakes his head. Takes the rifle from* JAMIE.]

JAMIE   Is she a terrorist too.

POWER   No.

154

JAMIE Good.

HEATHER What's going on here. [*To* JAMIE.] You're the General's new gardener. [*To* POWER.] What's he doing here.

JAMIE Moonlighting. I thought I'd earn a few extra bucks by offering to landscape this gentleman's campsite. Now if we put a few rocks over there –

POWER Shut up, Jamie. It's all right, Heather.

JAMIE Is she on our side.

POWER Yes.

JAMIE Good.

HEATHER I don't understand.

POWER He works for me.

JAMIE Actually I work *with* him. Can I get you a seat. Some coffee. How about something to eat.

POWER Good idea, Jamie. Cook us up a three-course meal. The stove's over there. [JAMIE *goes over and starts to putter around with the stove.*] What is it, Heather.

HEATHER Hackman called. You're invited to dinner tomorrow night.

POWER Good.

HEATHER He also grilled me for a while about how I knew you.

POWER Do you think he suspects you.

HEATHER No. He thinks I'm an airhead. That's why he bought all that crap about the local museum so easily. He suspects you though. But that might be all right. He thinks you're just down here to do a journalistic hatchet job on him.

JAMIE [*approaching them*]. That's the idea. Everything is right in place. I'm in place. Tyrone's in place. And now you're in place.

HEATHER Who is this guy, anyway.

JAMIE [*takes her hand*]. Jamie McLean. I'm his partner.

HEATHER Partner in what.

POWER We're still working out the details.

HEATHER Why didn't you tell me about him.

JAMIE Hey. That's his style. Close to the vest. You gotta respect it. It gets results. He didn't tell me about you either. What's your part in this.

POWER Heather is a friend of Paul Reinhardt's.

JAMIE Ahhh ... You were his girlfriend.

HEATHER What do you mean 'were'! Oh my God. You've found out that he's dead, haven't you Tyrone ... [*Staggers.*]

155

POWER Here, sit down. [*Helps her onto the camping-stool.*] Good work, Jamie.

JAMIE I'm sorry. [*Goes behind the tent. Sits.*]

HEATHER I knew. He had to be dead. He left me that night to sneak into Hackman's house. And when he didn't come back I knew. What else would Hackman do. How did you find out.

POWER I didn't. But I'm sure he is, Heather.

HEATHER But to get Hackman we have to prove it.

POWER We will.

JAMIE We will?

HEATHER How?

JAMIE Yeah, how?

POWER Patience. We'll let Hackman make some moves first. I want the larger picture of what he's up to. Paul would have wanted it that way.

HEATHER Ah come on, Tyrone. Paul was no crusader like you. He just wanted Hackman's balls on the line because it would have been a good story. He was a good reporter but he had no mission. Just get Hackman. I feel so damn guilty. It was me who tipped Paul off that Hackman was up to something.

POWER Why didn't you tell me that before.

HEATHER Because I thought my father might be involved. It was something I heard them talking about.

POWER Go ahead.

HEATHER My father. Can you leave him out of this.

POWER Should I?

HEATHER Jesus. I don't know. I think Hackman was after his help. I don't think my father was directly involved. Hackman just wanted money from him.

POWER Your father shares a lot of Hackman's views.

HEATHER Well they're from the same old world, Tyrone. But I think my father's ideas about how to sustain that world stop short of forming private armies and things like that.

JAMIE Private armies? I don't like the sound of that.

POWER That's why Mendez is in prison. He was forming a large illegal mercenary force. The rumour is that Hackman was a 'consultant'. Heather, what did Hackman want the money from your father for.

HEATHER I can't say for sure. I could speculate.

POWER Me too. Maybe to get someone out of prison in a foreign country? An operation like that could cost a lot of money.

HEATHER Simón Mendez.

POWER Simón Mendez. Yes.

HEATHER Right. That's what Paul thought too.

POWER Why.

HEATHER Because he found out Karla Mendez was staying with Hackman.

POWER For chrissake. Paul went into Hackman's place knowing that Karla Mendez was there. Was he insane.

HEATHER You're going there tomorrow night for dinner. Are you insane. [POWER *has wandered over to the cliff's edge. Is staring down.*]

JAMIE No he's on a mission.

POWER Not me. Hackman's the only one with a mission. And to make it he's got to play a dicey double-edged game. He's got to stay close enough to government circles to be useful to his fascist friends and that means convincing sceptics like me that he really is nothing more now than the insignificant adviser to an insignificant minister of culture. But at the same time he's got to make his moves. This operation doesn't begin or end with setting Mendez free. They're going to make some big insurgent move somewhere. He's afraid of me. Afraid of what I'll write. So he wants to talk cultural policy and convince me. I'll let him. And then maybe he'll think I'll write something that will convince everyone else. And then he'll make his moves with confidence. And then I'll get him. And I'll get Mendez. And I'll get everything they both stand for.

JAMIE But it's good to know you don't have a mission.

POWER There's something going on down there on the beach in front of Hackman's place. Hand me the rifle.

JAMIE No way. You've worked yourself into a frenzy, Power. You can't just shoot him.

POWER The telescopic sight is infrared.

JAMIE So what.

POWER It sees in the dark. It was the only way I could get one. I had to buy the whole rifle. Hand it over. [*Hands it to him.* POWER *looks through it.*]

JAMIE Well?...Well?

POWER It doesn't work. Nothing I buy ever works. Have you noticed that. That new typewriter I bought last month doesn't work.

JAMIE That 'new' typewriter is twelve years old.

POWER But I bought it. And it doesn't work. I bet it worked before I bought it. Life does things like that to people like me. Why is that. Why doesn't life do things like that to people like Hackman. Think about it. I want you to think about that. I'm going down there for a closer look. [*Leaves.*]

HEATHER You shouldn't let him go by himself.

JAMIE He likes to be alone when he's like this. He likes to ask himself questions like why does life do these things to me and he likes to give himself answers like because life is stupid, Power. Life doesn't know that you're the only person alive with his own moral code. The only person who can save the whole world from destruction and spiritual emptiness.

HEATHER It's from all those years in the newspaper business. It can do things to them. It made Paul reckless.

JAMIE [*checking the telescopic sight*]. It does work. You just have to adjust it. He's so lousy with mechanical things. I think he's in the wrong century. I'm sorry about Paul.

HEATHER Thanks.

JAMIE Had you been together a long time.

HEATHER We hadn't 'been together' at all.

JAMIE But Power said –

HEATHER No he didn't. He said I was his friend. And that's all I was. Just a good friend.

JAMIE Oh.... How did you meet Power.

HEATHER Through Paul. He taught a journalism course I took. Power used to lecture us sometimes.

JAMIE Was he tedious.

HEATHER Well let's just say he took his subject seriously. In fact it seemed to depress him. [*Takes a flask of whisky from her purse.*]

JAMIE Yeah, that's Power. If he knows about it, he's depressed about it. [*Notices the flask.*] Are you a journalist.

HEATHER Yes. [*Takes a drink.*] My father owns the local newspaper. I work for it.

JAMIE You work for your father. But you don't agree with his politics.

HEATHER He tolerates me. Maybe because he thinks I'm stupid. Like the General does. I don't mind. I'm biding my time. Someday the paper will be mine. And its politics will be mine too.

JAMIE And your politics are like Power's, I guess.

HEATHER Yeah. Sort of. What are yours.

JAMIE Ah, I don't know. All I know about politics is that it's depressing. It seems to suck the spontaneity right out of most people. And it makes others, like Power, well ... deranged.

HEATHER How did you meet him. Power.

JAMIE I was a janitor. I used to clean offices part-time while I was going to school. I cleaned his office. Have you ever seen his office. It was a mess. Just like him. Drunk all the time. Writing this dumb novel he's been trying to finish for about a hundred years. I changed his life. I cleaned his office and infected him with my contagious spirit. Do you sense my contagious spirit.

HEATHER It's overwhelming me.

JAMIE I like you. We'll be close, I can tell.

HEATHER That sounds like a threat.

JAMIE You'll learn to love it. Just like Power did. He's alive. Sure he doesn't make sense most of the time. But he's got spirit.

HEATHER And now he's got a mission.

JAMIE I think he thinks it's a war. That's why he dragged us down here a thousand miles. All the way on the train his eyes were funny and he was talking about the new world fascism and the military mind. And when we got here he got worse. Like he was smelling Hackman even before he met him. Like he was sniffing in the air for the enemy. It's so ironic on top of all that, Hackman being this cultural adviser thing. Power hates art. He thinks it's 'the leisurely reflection of a dying society.' Those are his words, not mine. It just twists and turns, this thing between him and Hackman. And it's growing. I'm beginning to feel it myself. It would be funny if Hackman really did care about culture, you know, the fascist who cares about culture. And Power wants to destroy him. But isn't culture a fine

159

thing. Isn't that what we're told. So it keeps twisting and turning this thing. It's got me thinking about it and I don't usually think about these things. I'm too smart. It kills you. But this is war. This is Power's war. And dammit, now I'm thinking about it too.

HEATHER So am I. [POWER *returns. Sombre-looking.*]

JAMIE Did you see anything down there.

POWER Death. I saw death down there. [*Takes a flask of whisky from a pocket. Drinks.*]
BLACKOUT

Scene Five

Later. The patio. Lit by several Japanese lanterns. BROWN *is looking around through a pair of binoculars.* KARLA *comes out.*

KARLA Where is he.

BROWN On the beach. [KARLA *mutters.*] How did your meeting at the airport go.

KARLA He agreed to help us.

BROWN You mean he agreed to let us pay him to help us. I notice you no longer have the briefcase.

KARLA I would like a drink please. [*There is a small, portable bar in a corner of the patio.* BROWN *leaves the binoculars on a chair, goes to the bar.*]

BROWN What would you like.

KARLA I don't care. [BROWN *makes a drink.* KARLA *picks up the binoculars. Looks through them.*] What's he doing down there.

BROWN Digging.

KARLA Why?

BROWN You'll have to ask him.

KARLA I'm asking you!

BROWN [*hands her the drink*]. I'm sorry you're upset, miss. The fact that your father's old friend took money from you must be hard for you to swallow. You don't understand the mercenary mind, miss.

KARLA   Your mind, Brown?

BROWN   I'm no mercenary, miss. I have a loyalty.

KARLA   To what.

BROWN   The general.

KARLA   It's strange how he attracts certain kinds of personalities to him.

BROWN   The general will set the world right, miss. The general and men like him.

KARLA   No. Men like my father will set the world right. Men like the general are their tools.

BROWN   Beg your pardon, miss, but your father's rotting in a South American prison. I don't remember the general ever getting himself in a position anything like that.

KARLA   He has a way of looking out for himself.

BROWN   No, miss. He's just not easily beguiled. [KARLA *mutters.* HACKMAN *comes on from the beach. Carrying a shovel.*]

HACKMAN   Good evening, Karla. You look upset. Didn't it go well.

KARLA   Well enough.

HACKMAN   Good. Brown, could you pour me one of those. A double.

BROWN   Sir. [*Goes to the bar.*]

KARLA   He said he'd have my father out within a week.

HACKMAN   Then why don't you look happy.

KARLA   I don't trust him.

HACKMAN   Because he took the money? Just because he's practical doesn't mean he can't be trusted. Relax. He'll get your father out because he knows if he doesn't I'll kill him. That's how the world works Karla. By contract. I thought you knew that. I thought that's what you believed in.

KARLA   I believe in my father.

HACKMAN   And your father believes in force. The force of contracts. [BROWN *hands* HACKMAN *his drink.*] Thank you.

BROWN   Did you retrieve it, sir?

HACKMAN   Yes.

KARLA   Retrieve what.

HACKMAN   [*Reaches into his pocket. Produces a small notebook.*] This. A journalist's notebook. You know, Brown, it would have been far less unpleasant to have searched him before we buried him.

BROWN   An unforgivable lapse, sir. I can only say that I must be out of practice.

KARLA   You killed someone.

HACKMAN   He was a trespasser. This is my property. I own it. I have a
deed. A contract. People in this world must learn that
certain things are inviolate. Besides, dear, he was spying
on us.

KARLA   So you are suspected.

HACKMAN   It appears so.

KARLA   Are there others.

HACKMAN   There is one other. A friend of the dead journalist. That's
why I retrieved the notebook. To see what he had written
down and possibly passed on to his friend. Mr. Power.
Brownie, do me a favour. Take a quick read through this
and brief me later.

BROWN   [*takes the notebook*]. I won't take long, sir.

HACKMAN   Take your time. Let's not let them panic us. Let's not
change our style, Brownie. They are the foolish ones,
remember. [BROWN *nods. Leaves.*] You know Karla I might
have to leave here. Run away. That would be sad. I like it
here. I like my garden. I like the ocean. I could have even
grown to like my new job. I do like artistic things, Karla.
Did you know that about me.

KARLA   No.

HACKMAN   Art is the leisurely reflection of an elite society. Who said
that.

KARLA   I don't know.

HACKMAN   Perhaps I just made it up then. I'm getting poetic in my
old age. Karla if I have to leave, we'll go together. We'll join
up with your father and work for his future success.
Would you like that.

KARLA   If it was a useful merger. You can be useful. I suppose.

HACKMAN   It could be like the old days. Panama City. Madrid. Places
in between. You are a woman I could love. [*Touches her
hair.*]

KARLA   You said that once before.

HACKMAN   You see? I never repeat myself unless I mean it. I must love
you. And somehow you must love me. [*Touches her neck.*]

KARLA   Don't ... [*Shrugs.*] Of what exactly are you suspected.

HACKMAN   Of helping you. And your father. Of helping to free a
charismatic right-wing lunatic who wants to change half
the world. Change it to a place where contracts are
honoured. And duty is done. And loyalty is kept. Change it
into our kind of world. [*Touches her cheek.*]

KARLA   I have no loyalty to you.

HACKMAN   But I've helped your father. Put myself in danger. And I may have to run. You could comfort a man on the run.

KARLA   Comfort, maybe. But that is not love.

HACKMAN   Let me be the judge of that. [*Grabs her.*]

KARLA   No.

HACKMAN   Let me. [*Puts his arms around her. Kisses her. She laughs.*]

KARLA   How do you plan to use me.

HACKMAN   How do you wish to be used. [*They kiss.*]

BLACKOUT

Scene Six

The beam of a flashlight. The sound of someone moving around, some metal clanging. Suddenly the flashlight is dropped. Darkness. A groan. A louder groan. A thud.
Pause. Lights.
We are in a small room in HACKMAN*'s house full of filing cabinets.* BROWN *is standing with his foot on* JAMIE*'s throat.* JAMIE *is lying on the floor in front of him.* HACKMAN *stands to the rear, hands in his pockets.*

BROWN   Don't move, laddie. If you move you die. Are you armed. Don't lie, laddie. If you lie you die. [JAMIE *shakes his head.*]

HACKMAN   Let him up.

BROWN   [*removes his foot*]. Up you get. [JAMIE *gets up slowly.*]

HACKMAN   Make him comfortable. [BROWN *picks* JAMIE *up and puts him on a filing cabinet. The filing cabinet is about four feet high.* HACKMAN *approaches* JAMIE. JAMIE *is rubbing his throat.*] Let's make it simple, shall we. We know you're not a gardener. We know you're an associate of Mr. Power's. We know you've been spying on us. All we don't know is why. And you're going to tell us that right now.

JAMIE   He paid me! I'm a paid lackey. I do anything for anyone who pays me. Would you like to pay me to spy on Power. No problem. I'll do it. Trust me.

BROWN   Shut up, laddie. [*Rubs his forehead.*]

HACKMAN   You're telling me you don't share his political beliefs.

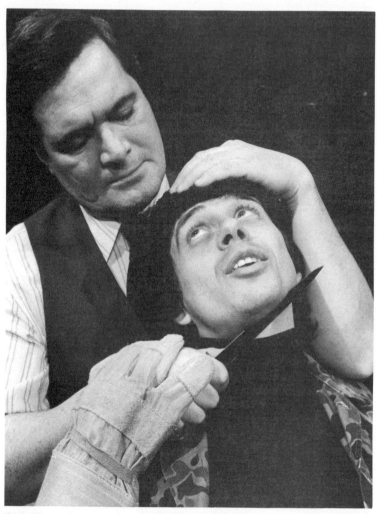

Dean Hawes (BROWNIE) and Jim Henshaw (JAMIE)

JAMIE   He's a washed-out liberal. Liberals, conservatives, communists, fascists. Who cares. Not me. I'm a working-class pragmatist. I believe in the politics of staying alive.

HACKMAN   Under the circumstances I would say that makes you quite idealistic. [*Nods at* BROWN. BROWN *pulls a stiletto from his sleeve. Places it at* JAMIE*'s throat.*]

BROWN   The man is telling you that you're not saying the things he wants to hear.

JAMIE   [*to* HACKMAN]. I'm just trying to say I'm not interested in your political involvement.

HACKMAN   My only political involvement is as cultural adviser.

JAMIE   Right. And I can help you there too. They say this country has no real working-class art. And I think that's because it's always presented by a bunch of middle-class academics who patronize the shit out of the working-class with a lot of romantic bullshit. Now, if you pay me enough, I could set up a study, hold regional meetings, write a report on my findings and –

BROWN   Please do shut up, laddie. [*Now rubbing his forehead furiously.*]

HACKMAN   Steady, Brown.

BROWN   I'll be all right, sir. [*Turns his back, goes to a corner.*]

JAMIE   Why is he always doing that. Rubbing his forehead like that.

BROWN   [*advancing*]. War wound! [HACKMAN *gets between them. Gestures.* BROWN *returns to his corner.*]

HACKMAN   Steel plate.

JAMIE   Steel plate?!

HACKMAN   Please. You'll embarrass him.

JAMIE   I'm sorry.

HACKMAN   Let's continue without him, all right?

JAMIE   Sure.

HACKMAN   Are you uncomfortable? Not too ill at ease?

JAMIE   No actually I'm starting to feel okay.

HACKMAN   Yes. Well that's a mistake. [HACKMAN *suddenly and viciously grabs* JAMIE*'s collar and throws him off the filing cabinet across the floor and into another filing cabinet.* JAMIE *slowly collapses to the floor.*] How are you feeling now.

JAMIE   How do you want me to feel.

HACKMAN   Scared.

JAMIE   Okay.

HACKMAN   Three questions. What were you looking for in my files. What did Power learn from Reinhardt. Has Power passed on anything he's learned to anyone else. [JAMIE *just looks at him*..]Answers. [*Kicks* JAMIE *in the side*].

JAMIE   [*groans*]. Okay. Stop. I've got something to say. [*Groans.*] But I gotta get up. [*Getting up slowly.*] I gotta be on my feet. [*Up.*] Okay, I'm up. [*Straightens, looks at* HACKMAN. *Inhales. Exhales.*] Go fuck yourself. [HACKMAN *hits him and* JAMIE *falls to the floor. Unconscious.* HACKMAN *is standing over* JAMIE.]

BROWN   [*joins him*]. I'm sorry you had to do that yourself, sir.

HACKMAN   It's all right, Brown. You were there in spirit.

BROWN   But a man like you shouldn't have to do things like that, sir. Those are things that a man like me should do. I've been letting you down quite a bit lately I'm afraid. It's the head. Always acts up at these times. I think it's the excitement. The promise of violence, if that doesn't sound too barbaric, sir.

HACKMAN   Not at all, Brown. You're a soldier. You have instincts. And this is war.

BROWN   Is it, sir.

HACKMAN   Oh yes, I think so.

BROWN   Have we lost it. Is that why we have to get out of the country.

HACKMAN   No that's something else. Something larger. A chance to prepare for the real war to come. This is something a bit unreal. This is a little war we have to fight before we go. A matter of conflicting points of view. This is a war between me and Mr. Power.

BROWN   I hated him on sight, sir. I hated his flabby belly. I hated all the books he'd read and the schools he'd gone to. Just like that. Without even knowing him.

HACKMAN   You know him. He's the enemy. The humanist. The egalitarian. The constant appeaser. He wants to turn the world into Jello. [*Points to* JAMIE.] And that's the enemy's spy. When he wakes up, do it again. And keep doing it until he talks. He has nothing to tell us but we should make him talk. It's a matter of principle. It's a battle of wills. His against ours.

BROWN	Not exactly an even battle, sir.
HACKMAN	I know. Sad, isn't it. It's a pathetic little war. But it's the only one we've got! [*Leaves.* BROWN *looks at* JAMIE. *Rubs his forehead. Advances.*]
	BLACKOUT

Scene Seven

The patio. POWER *and* HEATHER. *Drinks before dinner. They are dressed casually.* POWER *is pouring himself a glass of wine.*

HEATHER	Why are they keeping us waiting.
POWER	So we'll get nervous.
HEATHER	It's working. I'm starting to sweat. I don't know if I can go through with this.
POWER	Be strong. Have a drink.
HEATHER	No thanks. I'd rather stay alert. I think it would be good if you stayed alert too.
POWER	I'm just having enough to give me a fighting edge.
HEATHER	We should have called the police.
POWER	Nah. They'd ruin everything. Besides, vengeance is mine saith the Lord and since the Lord isn't here tonight I'm standing in for him. Vengeance, therefore, is mine. [BROWN *comes on. In a suit.*]
BROWN	Are you comfortable.
POWER	Absolutely. [HEATHER *smiles. Nods.*]
BROWN	[*to* HEATHER]. Would you like another cocktail.
POWER	No. I've just been helping myself to the wine.
BROWN	So I see. How unique to drink the wine before the dinner.
POWER	I was beginning to get afraid there wasn't going to be a dinner.
BROWN	Of course. Patience is the virtue of a confident man.
POWER	I don't know. I'm a confident man. And I'm just rarin' to go. [BROWN *starts off.*]
HEATHER	[*looks at* POWER]. Oh, Brown.
BROWN	[*stopping*]. Yes.

HEATHER Is your gardener around. I thought I might ask him about the mixture in my compost heap.

BROWN No. I'm sorry. He had a little accident. We had to send him away.

HEATHER [*stands*]. What kind of – [POWER *grabs her arm.*]

BROWN Something wrong, miss?...

POWER No. She's fine. [BROWN *nods. Leaves.*]

HEATHER They've killed Jamie. [POWER *stares into his glass.*] Tyrone. They've killed him. [POWER *doesn't respond. Just stares down.*] Tyrone. Do something.

POWER I will. [*Looks up.*] I will. [*Suddenly the patio is filled with music. A heart-pounding, lush, symphonic march. Very loud.* HEATHER *and* POWER *have to shout over the music.*]

HEATHER What the hell is that?

POWER Psychological warfare! [*Grimaces.*] Unbelievable! This guy is unbelievable! [HACKMAN *and* KARLA *enter. Arm-in-arm. Pose at the door and begin a slow regal walk to the table and around it once and then stop.* HACKMAN *is wearing a perfectly tailored tuxedo. Military ribbons on his chest.* KARLA *is wearing a black evening-gown. And a red sash with a small insignia on it.* POWER *and* HEATHER *are just staring at them.* HACKMAN *makes a subtle gesture and the music stops. And simultaneously* BROWN *is there with a camera to take a picture of* KARLA *and* HACKMAN. BROWN *leaves. Pause.*]

HEATHER Quite an entrance.

HACKMAN Thank you. We were aiming for something stylish.

POWER Unbelievable.

HACKMAN Too much, do you think?

POWER Oh no. It was just right. I had an orgasm. [*To* HEATHER.] How about you.

HEATHER No. Sorry.

POWER I think she probably likes more foreplay. But for me, the earth moved. It really did.

HACKMAN If you're finished, I'll make the introductions.

POWER Of course, how moronically rude of me to keep the charming lady waiting. [*Stands.*] And she's wearing her favourite battle dress, too.

HACKMAN Mr. Power. Heather Masterson. Allow me to present Karla Mendez.

POWER [*kisses her hand*]. Daughter of Simón Mendez. Widely known banker and ultra-conservative patron of the political movement affectionately known as 'lunatics for a better world.'

KARLA [*sits*]. Are you drunk, Mr. Power.

POWER A bit, perhaps.

KARLA Then it would be wise if you watched your tongue.

HACKMAN [*sits*]. It's all right Karla. Mr. Power has what he considers to be an original conversational style. Even though to others, it may seem more like the rantings of a desperately under-equipped intellect. In any event I think we should not respond to him too hastily nor take him too seriously.

POWER There are parts of that speech I actually agree with. You gotta guess which ones though. [KARLA *and* HACKMAN *laugh.* POWER *and* HEATHER *frown and slump in their chairs.*]

HACKMAN How are you this evening, Heather.

HEATHER What is the purpose of this dinner party, General.

HACKMAN To eat. To make conversation.

POWER To strike a deal.

HACKMAN Yes. Perhaps later to even strike a deal.

HEATHER I think it stinks. If we've got things to say let's say them.

HACKMAN This is my house, Heather. We'll do this my way. You've changed, Heather. You're not the little girl I used to know.

HEATHER I never was. I've hated your kind all my life.

HACKMAN Well you've been very good at keeping it a secret. Was this so that you could spy on me.

HEATHER Yes.

HACKMAN For whom.

HEATHER Friends.

HACKMAN Like Mr. Power here. No. Not Mr. Power himself, of course. People like him though. Of his ilk, so to speak.

HEATHER If that means people who believe in things like a free press and elections and ... and ...

POWER Peace.

HEATHER Peace. Well yeah then, yeah.

HACKMAN You're still a child, Heather. Naive and self-righteous.

HEATHER And you're a murdering son-of-a-bitch. And I'm not going a bit farther with this crap. [*Stands.*] I'm going for the police.

Diane D'Aquila (KARLA) and David Fox (HACKMAN)

KARLA   I think you should sit down, little girl.

HEATHER   Don't little girl me. I know your story. You throw bombs at people to get what you want. And you've already got three million dollars in a Swiss bank. You're just a common greedy criminal. [KARLA *is muttering furiously.*]

HACKMAN   Mr. Power, explain to her why she should sit down.

POWER   The general has a pistol under his jacket.

HEATHER   So what?

HACKMAN   The full sentence should have been 'The general has a pistol under his jacket which he will use.'

POWER   Sit down, Heather. Our time is coming.

HACKMAN   It's here now, Mr. Power. I'm afraid Heather has ruined the mood for dinner. I was prepared to dazzle you with my suggestions for a cultural policy. But of course that sham will be unnecessary.

POWER   You got any other shams you want to try out?

HACKMAN   I have your friend, Mr. Power. I have him and it's up to you to get him back.

POWER   He's alive?

HACKMAN   More or less.

POWER   If you've hurt him I'll –

HACKMAN   Oh please, Mr. Power, you'll what? Lash me with your tongue? Write a nasty article about me? Put my name on a petition and send it to all your friends?

POWER   That's not a bad idea. Ban the Fascist.

HACKMAN   An unfortunate choice of words, in the modern context, I mean. I'm someone who just wants to rid the world of chaos, get the economy moving again, and restore order.

POWER   General, I've been waiting all my life to say this to someone like you. [*Stands.*] Any asshole can get the trains running on time!! Any asshole can do that, but it takes something more to get the people on the trains for any reason other than the fact that they're scared shitless of the asshole who got them running on time. And another thing. It's too bad you didn't get a chance to infect me with your contrived ideas on culture because I was ready for that too.

HACKMAN   Strangely enough my ideas on culture are quite sincere.

POWER   Oh I bet they are. All concerned with harmony and beauty and the glorious heart within. That piece of schlock that

171

accompanied your musical ride into dinner was probably a good example.

HACKMAN You would have preferred an earthy folk song, no doubt. [POWER *is fuming.* HEATHER *is gesturing him on.* KARLA *and* HACKMAN *are shaking their heads. Muttering.*]

POWER That's it. That's the point! I wouldn't have preferred. I don't *dictate.* If you'll pardon the pun. Culture is like everything else. Just is. It evolves out of just being. Like everything else. Like society. A changing society. An evolving society! Oh God Almighty I want you dead and rotting in the ground!! And if I could I'd reach back into history and remove every trace of every person you have anything in common with and right all the wrong they've done in the name of all that is brutal and elitist and just plain goddamn vicious and greedy! [*In one quick move* KARLA *pulls a small pistol from under her dress, stands, points the gun at* POWER *and shoots.* HEATHER *yells. Pause.*] Am I shot? [*Checking his body.*] Am I shot? [*To* HEATHER.] See any blood? I don't feel anything. Maybe I'm in shock. Maybe I'm dying.

HACKMAN Brutal, elitist, vicious, greedy, but decisive, Mr. Power? Quite decisive?

POWER Well am I dying or not. Isn't anyone going to tell me.

KARLA I aimed wide.

POWER Thanks. [*Sits.*]

KARLA Next time I won't. John, I think the little girl was right. Must we go on with this. This man is intolerable.

HACKMAN But just a little bit amusing, no?

KARLA No. Intolerable and tiring. Very tiring. And we have a long journey ahead of us tomorrow.

HEATHER Going away for good, General.

HACKMAN I'm afraid so. I'm afraid your friend Mr. Reinhardt has probably made it impossible for me to stay.

HEATHER You killed him. You killed him but he got you. For sure he got the word out that Miss Murder here was your guest and people will put that together with whatever you're planning to do to help her father.

HACKMAN Well I can't be sure, but I can't take any chances either. We do have a meeting with destiny, you know.

POWER What about us.

HACKMAN	You have a meeting with your own destiny, Mr. Power.
POWER	Ah yes. The vast darkness. Chaos and death.
HACKMAN	I hope to make it a clean death, Mr. Power. No chaos. Just a bullet. I was hoping to play with you some more but you're too boring. Besides, you have nothing I want and all you want from me is to listen to you rant. It really is a pathetic little war, Mr. Power. No thunder. No lightning.
POWER	[*Has his hands under the table. Is leaning forward.*] I have a little lightning under the table, General. It's a thirty-eight calibre special. And it's pointed straight at you.
KARLA	He's lying.
POWER	Try going. Find out.
HACKMAN	It doesn't matter. Brown probably heard that shot. He'll be coming in soon, Mr. Power. And no mere thirty-eight is going to stop him.
POWER	He'll just walk into it, right. He'll march into his death for you.
HACKMAN	Try him. Find out. In the meantime, perhaps it's a standoff.
HEATHER	What do we do.
POWER	I'm thinking. [*Long pause.*]
KARLA	John. He's bluffing.
HACKMAN	We'll see soon enough.
HEATHER	Tyrone.
POWER	I'm thinking. [*Long pause. The sound of footsteps. Someone approaching. They all look. Pause.* JAMIE *stumbles in. His face bloodied. Limping.*] Jamie.
JAMIE	Power. He beat the shit out of me. Old Killer Eyes. He's a mean bastard.... Power, help me ... Power [*Falls.* HACKMAN *makes a move to get up, but* POWER *stands.* POWER *does have a gun. He grabs* KARLA *and puts the gun to her head, while almost simultaneously* HACKMAN *is doing the same thing to* HEATHER. JAMIE *is struggling to get to his feet.*]
HACKMAN	This looks like a standoff for sure.
POWER	Can you get up, Jamie.
JAMIE	Yeah. [*Struggling up.*] He hurt me. He came back to hurt me some more but ... his head started to bother him pretty bad and I knocked him down and pushed a filing cabinet on top of him.
POWER	Don't worry, Heather. We'll get you out.

HACKMAN Not by going to the police, Mr. Power. That would mean she dies. I promise you that.

POWER Get up, Jamie. We're leaving.

JAMIE [*On his feet. Staggering.*] Yeah ... sure ... great idea. Old Killer Eyes is lying under a filing cabinet. He looks real stupid. But he's not dead ... kind of wish he was. God he hurt me.

POWER Get going. I'm right behind you. [JAMIE *starts off.* POWER *is backing up. Holding* KARLA.]

POWER Is this better, General. Is this a better quality war. I mean now we've both got prisoners. Exciting, eh.

HEATHER For chrissake, Power. I don't much feel like sacrificing myself so you can get your rocks off.

HACKMAN Yes. Why make the ladies suffer. How about a prisoner exchange.

POWER That's not how it's done, General. Even I know that. You don't exchange prisoners in the enemy's camp. You find a neutral territory.

HACKMAN Where.

POWER You'll hear from me.

JAMIE Where am I.

POWER Just keep going.

JAMIE Where.

POWER Left foot. Right foot. Leave the rest to me.

JAMIE [*in a daze*]. Left foot. Right foot. Left ... [JAMIE, POWER *and* KARLA *are gone.* HACKMAN *lowers his gun. Lets go of* HEATHER.]

HEATHER He'll go to the police.

HACKMAN I don't think so. That would spoil his fun.

HEATHER What is this. Are you two playing some kind of game or something.

HACKMAN He is, I think. But not me. And that's the basic difference between us which Mr. Power will soon find out about. [BROWN *comes on. Soiled. Walking slowly.*]

BROWN How did it go.

HACKMAN More or less as planned. Your part as well, I gather.

BROWN I think I gave a brilliant performance, if I may say so, sir.

HACKMAN Did he hurt you.

BROWN The fool threw an empty filing cabinet on me. Wouldn't hurt a fly. The kid thinks he's real tough.

HACKMAN They both do, Brown. They both do. [*Laughs. Picks up a glass of wine. Drinks. Laughs again.*] I love this!
BLACKOUT

Scene Eight

Dawn. In different areas, eventually all merging into one. The campsite on the cliff. KARLA *is sitting on a campstool. Her hands tied behind her back.* POWER *is kneeling next to* JAMIE, *washing the blood from his face.*

POWER Does it hurt?
JAMIE Yeah.
POWER I was right about Hackman, wasn't I. He's nuts.
JAMIE Yeah. You were right.
POWER [*shrugs*]. Yeah. Well good for me. I guess. What possessed you to sneak in there in the first place.
JAMIE You. Your disease. Whatever you've got I had for a while.
POWER But you don't have it anymore.
JAMIE Killer Eyes knocked some sense into me. Power, I think we should call the authorities.
POWER No. This is my job.
JAMIE Really. Who gave it to you.
POWER Look. I'm sorry this happened to you but –
JAMIE No you're not. You're not even here. What is it exactly you want from Hackman. I've got to know, Power. I feel like I've been run over by a truck and I hate thinking there's no reason for it.
POWER I want him dead.
JAMIE Really? No metaphors? You don't mean in a larger spiritual way. You know how you usually talk? You mean really dead?
POWER Yeah.
JAMIE Why? Because he killed your friend Paul Reinhardt?
POWER Sure. That's a good reason. There are others of course.
JAMIE Of course. [*Shakes his head.*] Are *you* going to kill him, Power.

175

POWER   If I get the chance.

JAMIE   You can't. It's not in you.

POWER   Oh I think it is. I've got a feeling.

JAMIE   You've been drinking again.

POWER   Yeah. To make the feeling go away. But it won't. [*Picks up the rifle. Wanders over to the cliff's edge.*]

JAMIE   Is it a scary feeling?

POWER   Yeah.

KARLA   I wouldn't worry. I doubt if you'll get the chance to do anything about it.

JAMIE   I'm not in love with her anymore. [*To* KARLA.] I used to love you from a distance. When I got closer I noticed you had serious flaws in your personality.

KARLA   That is preferable, is it not, to having no personality at all.

JAMIE   You can't insult me. You and your buddies are just about finished. My friend here is a formidable opponent. Aren't you Power. [POWER *is looking through the sight, pointing the rifle down toward* HACKMAN*'s house.*] Aren't you, Power.

POWER   [*looks at him*]. I don't know. [*Lights out on this area. Lights up on the patio.* BROWN *is sitting there. In commando gear. Loading a rifle. Looking off toward the cliff.*]

BROWN   Come on, laddies. Come on down. Be tough. Be big tough boys. [*Rubs his forehead furiously.*] Oh man. I'm getting that old barbaric feeling. We're waiting, laddies. Won't you please come down. [*Rubs his forehead. Then raises the rifle to check the sight. Lights out on this area. Lights up on the beach.* HACKMAN *is sitting on a rock.* HEATHER *is digging a hole with a shovel.*]

HEATHER   What am I digging.

HACKMAN   A grave.

HEATHER   Whose?

HACKMAN   Well it's not mine.

HEATHER   It's pretty sick to make a person dig her own grave.

HACKMAN   How pessimistic, Heather. No, you're just not the same little girl I used to know. Journalism has dulled your imagination. Your friend Power is probably watching you dig. Do you suppose he's come to the same conclusion.

HEATHER   [*stops digging*]. You're baiting him.

HACKMAN   [*waves his gun*]. Keep digging, Heather.

HEATHER   You're a sadistic murdering bastard.

Scene Eight

HACKMAN Would you like to hear the speech on culture I prepared for Mr. Power.

HEATHER Not really.

HACKMAN Well you're going to hear it anyway. I worked too hard on it for it to go to waste.... Art. Art is the leisurely reflection of a discriminating society. Classical art is the historical reminder of earlier discrimination. The best art is the art of superficial spectacle which demonstrates the beauty of art for art's sake. [*Lights start to fade.*] Give five discriminating artists enough money to create five superficial spectacles and you will have a definition of a nation's culture. Culture? Culture is ... oh ... Culture is ... [*Lights out on this area. Lights up on the campsite.*]

POWER [*looking through the sight, the gun pointed down at the beach*]. I've got to get down there. [*Hands rifle to* JAMIE.] Here, take this. Watch her.

JAMIE You don't look well.

POWER I can't win. I just realized that.

JAMIE Then don't go.

POWER I have to get Heather away from him. But dammit. I can't win. Even if I get him. He's the only one who can win. Violence is his way, not mine. Life is always doing things like this to me. Have you ever noticed that. Think about it. [*Leaving.*]

JAMIE Be careful.

POWER I don't understand. Why me. I must be doing something wrong. I wonder what it is. [POWER *is gone.*]

KARLA He has no chance at all. [*Laughs.*]

JAMIE A momentary loss of faith. A little moral crisis. he has them all the time. [*Looks at the rifle.*] I hate guns. [KARLA *laughs.* JAMIE *looks at her.* KARLA *laughs louder. Lights out on this area. Lights up on the patio.* BROWN *has the rifle to his shoulder and is pointing it towards the cliff.*]

BROWN [*sings*].
　　　There once was a man called Power
　　　Who set himself up in a tower
　　　But when someone shot him
　　　They all soon forgot him
　　　And dead, Power decayed and turned sour.
　　　[*He laughs, then sings.*]

177

Getting to know you
Getting to know all about you.
Getting to like you
Getting to hope you like me.
[*Laughs.*] Come on down, laddie. That's it. Here he comes.
Are you ready, Sergeant. Yes sir. How do you feel Sergeant.
[*Rubs his forehead.*] Ooh. There's a pain I can live with, sir.
A real burden of love. [*The lights start to fade. He sings.*]
That old black magic's got me
In its spell.
That old black magic that we
Love so well.
[*Lights out on this area. Lights up on the beach.*]

HACKMAN   Opera. Opera is an example of what I mean. Many people think opera is a wasteful and irrelevant art form. But I believe its strength lies in its wastefulness. Its arrogant belief in its own –

HEATHER   Shut up! Will you please shut up. Shoot me. Strangle me. But please don't make me listen to any more of this garbage.

HACKMAN   [*waves his gun*]. Just keep digging. [*Four rifle shots.*]

HEATHER   What was that.

HACKMAN   The first two shots froze Mr. Power in his tracks with fear. The third shot blew off his foot. He of course fell down. The fourth shot hit him in the shoulder. He is dying. Very slowly. With plenty of time to think. I have a picture of it in my head. Very finely etched. Very tasteful, in its own way. A very creative ending. Not only does he get to watch his own death, but from where he's lying he can see yours too.

HEATHER   You're insane.

HACKMAN   Please. Say something more original. Something creative. Because it will certainly be the last thing you'll ever say. [*Lifts his gun.*]

HEATHER   Mr. Power has his gun pointed at your back.

HACKMAN   Well, that's creative. But it's not very original.

POWER   [*Walking out of the darkness. Holding his gun with both hands.*] I think she was going for the documentary approach. [HACKMAN *smiles.*] Get his gun. [HEATHER *grabs* HACKMAN's *gun.*] Turn around.

HACKMAN   What are you going to do now.

178

POWER   I'm thinking.

HEATHER   Do you know what this is, General. This is justice. You
murdered Paul Reinhardt and now you're going to pay.
Hooray for us, Power. I'll go call the police. [*Runs off.*]

HACKMAN   Now's your chance. All you have to do is pull the trigger.

POWER   Maybe there's another choice. I could hold you for the
police.

HACKMAN   No. If you don't shoot I'm leaving. I'll be gone, out of the
country before the police arrive.

POWER   Where can you go. There are international police
agencies. And extradition treaties.

HACKMAN   Where I'm going I can't be touched. I'm going to burrow
just beneath the surface of a foreign society. You'll know
I'm around though. Occasionally you'll read something in
a newspaper. A story about a return to order somewhere.
The setting of things right. And you'll know I've been
working.... Well, Mr. Power? Can you kill me?

POWER   I'm thinking. [*Lights out on this area. Lights up on patio.*
BROWN *is sprawled unconscious in a chair.* JAMIE *is standing
over him. Looking in a daze at his rifle.*]

HEATHER   [*runs on*]. What happened?

JAMIE   He was aiming for Power. He was going to shoot him. I saw
it all through this telescopic sight. I had to stop him.

HEATHER   You killed him?

JAMIE   I tried. I missed. Three times I missed. The fourth time I
hit that lantern and it fell on his head. He's unconscious. I
hate violence. I really do. This is not private-eye work.
Private eyes don't use rifles. They take divorce cases. And
make money. There's no money in this. There's only
misery in this. Where's Power.

HEATHER   On the beach. With Hackman.

JAMIE   Are you all right. I've been worried about you. I know we
just met but I felt we made a psychic connection. I'm
sensitive that way, you know.

HEATHER   [*touches his cheek*]. I'm all right. What about you. You
seem to be in a daze.

JAMIE   I am. I just tried to kill someone. I've never done that
before. I think it changed my life. [*Sits.*]

HEATHER   You better get down to the beach. Power might need your
help.

JAMIE   Helping Power makes me miserable. I just tried to kill

David Bolt (T.M. POWER) and Susan Purdy (HEATHER)

someone to help Power. It's a habit I've got to break.

HEATHER This is no time to go soft. This isn't defeat. This is victory. Justice. These guys killed Paul Reinhardt.

JAMIE Politics.

HEATHER No. Murder.

JAMIE No. War. Yes. I'm seeing it all now. I'm seeing how it works. I'm learning. This is a battle between two men. One of them, Power, wants the world to work properly with justice and equality and all those things. The other one, Hackman, just wants the world to work. Period. I figured all that out a while ago but I couldn't figure out my part in it all. But I learned. Experience taught me. I'm a pacifist. Will you marry me.

HEATHER What.

JAMIE I know you like me. I want to get married. Have children. Buy a small farm someplace. Will you marry me.

HEATHER No.

JAMIE Is that your final answer.

HEATHER This isn't the time. Power might be in danger. And there's something I'm supposed to be doing. I'm supposed to be calling the police. [*Starts off.*] Hey ... Hey. I liked you better when you had spirit. [*Leaves.*]

JAMIE Pacifists have spirit. I know. I can sense it growing inside me. A great spirit.

BROWN [*Groans. The groan turns into the first note of 'As Time Goes By'.*]

You must remember this
A kiss is still a kiss
A sigh is just a sigh
The fundamental things apply
As time goes by.

JAMIE [*in a daze, joining in*].

and when two lovers woo ... [*Continues.*]

BROWN [*sits up suddenly. Sees* JAMIE. *Advances.* JAMIE *raises two sets of fingers in the peace sign.* BROWN *sees this. Recoils. Rubbing his head furiously, he wanders off. And together he and* JAMIE *continue to sing. Fade out. Lights up on the beach.* POWER *is pointing the gun at* HACKMAN. *Thinking. Rubbing his head. Mumbling to himself. Gesturing.* HACKMAN *is looking at him curiously.* KARLA *appears. Walking quietly, slowly up behind* POWER.]

HACKMAN   No, don't bother him. He's thinking.

KARLA   About what? [POWER *turns. Caught between them. The gun moving from one to the other.*]

HACKMAN   The sanctity of life, probably. The moral implications of taking action. The pros. The cons. The pros. The cons. Ad infinitum, right, Mr. Power.

POWER   How did you escape.

KARLA   I got mad. It's easy if you get mad.

HACKMAN   She's right. Perhaps you should try getting mad, Mr. Power.

POWER   I am. [*And now* HACKMAN *and* KARLA *advance slowly.*]

HACKMAN   No. You're indignant. You're outraged. You just don't understand, do you. Anger is a weapon. Allowing you to be brutal. Brutality is another weapon. Allowing you to take action. In this way, you build your arsenal. Until you have the ultimate weapon. Immorality. Which allows you to take any action in any way at any time. Immorality is a great weapon. And you don't have it.

POWER   I don't need it. I've got a gun. See?

HACKMAN   So what.

POWER   I just thought it was a good time to remind you.

HACKMAN   The point is, you can't use it.

POWER   Just because I can't use it, doesn't mean I won't use it.

KARLA   What is he talking about.

HACKMAN   The gun is philosophically confusing to Mr. Power. Perhaps you could do him a favour and take it away from him. [KARLA *moves toward* POWER.]

POWER   Stay put.

KARLA   That's impossible. To take the gun I have to be closer.

POWER   Stop right there.

KARLA   One more step. [*Takes a step. Stops.*]

POWER   Be careful.

KARLA   All right. [*Pulls a fancy move. Kicks the gun out of* POWER's *hand. Picks it up.*]

POWER   Shit. I knew she was going to do that. I hate myself.

HACKMAN   No chance, Power. You had no chance. She hates you. She'd risk everything to beat you. You have to risk taking action! Let's go, Karla. It's over. [*Starts off.*]

KARLA   Almost. [*Shoots* POWER. POWER *drops to his knees. Holding his shoulder.*]

HACKMAN Did you do that for me.

KARLA [*walking past him*]. No. [*Leaves. Muttering.*]

HACKMAN Power ... Power?

POWER What?

HACKMAN Don't die. Try to live. It would be more interesting if you lived and we met again. There's so much I could teach you. [POWER *is trying to get to his feet.*] No. Please. No need to stand on my account. Besides, I want to remember you just as you are. [*Smiles. Pats* POWER *on the head. Leaves, humming an aria.* POWER *struggles to his feet. Turns in a circle. Falls on his rump.*]

POWER This is very, very depressing. [JAMIE *runs on.*]

JAMIE Power? Power.

POWER Over here.

JAMIE [*rushes over*]. What happened.

POWER You tied Karla's hands, didn't you.

JAMIE Yeah.

POWER You did a lousy job.

JAMIE Oh my God. You're shot.

POWER She shot me. She got loose because you didn't tie her up properly and she came down here and shot me. Why can't you do anything properly. Why can't *we* do anything properly. It's so goddamn depressing.

JAMIE Does it hurt.

POWER Yes.

JAMIE It looks bad.

POWER I could have killed him. But I didn't. I just thought about it. You're right about me. I think too much. Thinking doesn't help.

JAMIE Power. It looks really bad. Your wound is serious.

POWER I'll be all right. You better get after them. Karla and Hackman. They're getting away.

JAMIE I can't leave you. You're wounded. You may be dying.

POWER No. I'm not. Get going. You can at least try to follow them.

JAMIE [*Cradling* POWER's *head. Rocking back and forth.*] I can't. You're dying.

POWER I'm not dying.

JAMIE Yes you are.

POWER No I'm not. Get going. Let go of me.

JAMIE Oh my God, Power. You're dying.

POWER Dammit. Dammit. Dammit. I am not dying. Let me go. Get after them.

JAMIE I'm sorry, Power. I'm so sorry. Don't die. Don't die.

POWER I'm not. I'm not. [*Lights start to fade.*]

JAMIE It's so bad. It's so awful. Don't die.

POWER I can't stand it. They're getting away. We're letting them get away. We're failing again. I can't stand it. It's killing me.

JAMIE You're dying.

POWER No, it's killing me.

JAMIE You're dying.

POWER It's so depressing.

JAMIE Please don't die.

POWER For God's sake I'm not dying. I'm just depressed. It's just so damn depressing ... Jamie?

JAMIE What?

POWER We have to do better in the future. Promise me next time you tie someone up you'll do it properly.

JAMIE I promise.

POWER And I promise next time I go to war I'll win.... Or at least try to break even. I'm tired of losing. It's so ... depressing.
[JAMIE *is rocking back and forth.* POWER *is shaking his head.* HEATHER *runs on. Goes to them. Kneels. Suddenly they all look up. And on the cliff* KARLA, BROWN *and* HACKMAN *are looking down. Waving.*]
END